STARVE THE
VULTURE

STARVE THE VULTURE
A MEMOIR

BY JASON CARNEY

KAYLIE JONES BOOKS

ALSO AVAILABLE FROM KAYLIE JONES BOOKS
UNMENTIONABLES BY LAURIE LOEWENSTEIN
FOAMERS BY JUSTIN KASSAB
SING IN THE MORNING, CRY AT NIGHT BY BARBARA J. TAYLOR
THE LOVE BOOK BY NINA SOLOMON
WE ARE ALL CREW BY BILL LANDAUER
LITTLE BEASTS BY MATTHEW MCGEVNA (FORTHCOMING)

Published by Akashic Books
©2015 Jason Carney

ISBN-13: 978-1-61775-301-5
Library of Congress Control Number: 2014907317

First printing

Kaylie Jones Books
www.kayliejonesbooks.com

Akashic Books
Twitter: @AkashicBooks
Facebook: AkashicBooks
E-mail: info@akashicbooks.com
Website: www.akashicbooks.com

This book is dedicated to:

LCC
OCC
SCC
ECC

And your very flesh shall be a great poem.
—Walt Whitman

*It was just one dusk in an eternity
of fireflies and casual cruelty.*
—Philip Brady

APRIL 2007
3:10 A.M.
(00:05 BEFORE GRACE)

THE RED LIGHT TURNS GREEN. A surreal silence descends. I flick off the ignition and fixate on the body on the concrete. Only the smoke rising over this confusion seems peaceful in the aftermath. The debris field is a swirling cloud, a chaotic symphony gone silent like a pulse at the end of a phrase. The ease with which metal mangles is astounding. A one-car eruption that should have been two-car tragedy—I realize how close we came to a full-force impact.

He missed my car by inches!

I didn't see this coming, despite the sense of doom I've felt on the horizon since my mother's funeral. Every bad decision since I left the cemetery brought me to this moment. I don't know what to do. I'm disoriented by this unreal reality.

This shit just really happened!

Old Fingernails and I, distracted by our own bullshit, stuck at the intersection. The wreck ran up our backside at eighty miles an hour, the automobile screaming past us. The lift of the front end as the car cartwheeled, the massive cloud of damage that would have consumed my life, if not for his last-second decision to veer.

How are we not dead?

Without thinking, I open the door.

"Get back in the car! Let's go! Fuck that, dude!" Fingernails yells at me.

I sprint the forty feet to the body, my mind absent of the crack, the pipe, and the hooker with a purseful of dope in the front seat of my car. All my thoughts are of death. The feeling of impending disaster returns as I remember my mother's corpse. I remember the softness of her hair, each strand flowing and fragile next to the stiffness of her face dolled up in a coffin.

How did I avoid this accident?

He is young, no more than twenty-five. Lanky and white, his body covered in black-and-white tattoos. A speed pipe's bulbous end hangs out of his cutoff shorts' pocket and one flip-flop sandal with a broken strap clings to the flesh between his toes. His eyes roll wildly, unsure if his head still connects to his body.

"Don't move," I say. "Stay very still, you're all right."

"White boy, get back here!" yells the hooker.

There is no blood on him, not even a drop. All his limbs are in apparent working order, his breathing does not sound obstructed. I shake my head in amazement.

How could you live through that shit? Something or someone is looking out for us.

"Thank you for not hitting me," I say, retrieving the speed pipe from his pocket and tossing it to the ground. The glass shatters, camouflaged by the wreckage. "You're a lucky bastard."

"I've got 911!" a man yells from outside his truck across the street. "They just did a hit-and-run down at Peavey and Ferguson."

I envision this asshole chasing after the other car, trying to play hero with a cell phone.

"Put your shirt under his head," a voice in front of me instructs.

There is a woman standing on the sidewalk. I stare at her, wondering when she appeared. White with blond hair, she seems fit and well fed. Her skin brims with the healthy glow of a successful middle-aged life, her clothes pressed, her hair glossy. She does not belong around here. Without questioning her, I take off my orange T-shirt, ball it up, and place it under his head. Something sparks in his eyes as I cradle the back of his skull; a convulsion shakes his torso as if his lungs are underwater. Then a consciousness takes hold of him, faintly. His pupils enlarge and shrink as he struggles to focus.

"You're okay, brother. You're gonna be okay," I say, slowly and clearly. "Stay down, brother, wait for the fire trucks."

"The police are coming!" the man by the truck shouts. I turn to find the asshole already driving off.

I look to the woman on the sidewalk for further direction. *Where did she go?*

The spot on the sidewalk where she stood fills with a small group of onlookers, filing out of the crack-shamble apartments and duplexes on the street behind us. Sleep and euphoria cloud their eyes.

"White boy, the police are coming, let's go!" Fingernails yells.

The young man tries to rise up off the concrete. I position my hand over his chest.

"You got to stay down, your back might be messed up. Just stay down."

There's a tattoo on his left pectoral muscle; the delicate loops and bends of the letters scrawl the name *Debbie*.

That's my mother's name.

I am supposed to be here at this moment. But I don't want to know this. I don't want to face this. In a panic, I stand to return to my car and catch something out of the corner of my eye. It's a figure hanging upside down in the wreckage. My gut lurches.

"My friend's in the car," the man on the ground says, relaxing his body against the glass and loose gravel of the roadway.

"Stay down!"

"White boy!"

The totality of the situation floods over me, the wrong place at the right time. This is the moment I saw on the horizon my whole drugged-out life. I am content in the knowledge that addiction ends in an accidental overdose. I see it clearly: either I jump off the cliff or step back from the edge. There is no last time as long as next time is the last. This moment of choice was never a car wreck. Not a near miss.

Heavenly Father ...

The voice of my great-grandfather fills my head. There is a prayer dangling at the tip of my tongue, a plea to God that has not passed my lips since my mother's death three months ago. A congested, complicated series of images flashes across my brain. The dark red velvet cushions of the pews in the chapel of our family church, the sweet fragrance of the wildflowers decorating its front. The drum I broke at four. The first time my father hit my mom. The Icees that came in miniature Major League Baseball batting helmets from the Stop-n-Go corner store. The face of Mrs. Williams who still runs the day care I attended. The family dinner we had after my baptism at Mamaw and Papaw's house, a few blocks from this spot. The deep connection I hold with this neighborhood; both it and I caught up in the fantastic display of the wreck. The course of my days that brought me here, to this neighborhood, to this wreck, to myself, all three in shambles.

I look over at the upside-down car. A limb hangs out the window like a question mark. The reason I am still here among the wreckage.

... protect this man, ease his pain.

UNDER THE WATER
1976

THE WATER BITES MY LINGERING FEET at the top step.
The bottom of the white choir robe, big enough for a large
woman, floats out along the surface. A balloon halos around
my body. I look like a jellyfish. The preacher, water up to his
chest, stares out into the congregation, a forced smile on his
face. He extends an arm, nods his head. My mind is still in
the changing room, unsure if this is a good decision. The cold
makes him impatient. Silence fills the sanctuary. My family is
proud, occupying the first three rows, but I cannot see them
from where I stand. I imagine the preacher is looking in their
direction, wondering why their kin is not getting into the water.

I stare blankly at his robe. I see his chest hairs matted
against his wet body. I am scared the congregation will see
through my robe, and notice I am not wearing underwear.

Why didn't I bring a change of underwear?

I forget what my duties are in this situation, so I stand
there waiting for him to tell me.

"We gather to bring another young lamb unto our Heavenly Father. In the name of His son, Jesus Christ," the preacher
speaks to the crowd.

I remember why I decided to do this thing in the first
place. My father left when I was four, and after waiting two
years for him to come back, having a new father sounded like
a good idea. I am tired of waiting for my real father to show

up. The idea of my mom finding a man to replace him makes me uneasy. Big Brothers and Sisters had two and half years to come up with a weekend buddy, but they were too over-extended to help boys my age. A Heavenly Father is the best idea I came up with to fill the hole in my life.

Observant in Sunday school, I pay attention when the teacher speaks of our Heavenly Father and His constant presence in our lives. The whole thing sounds magical. Besides, I remember my family gave Craig gifts and a dinner party the day of his baptism.

I wonder what valuables I will obtain today.

"He's a little nervous," the preacher says to the congregation. Some quietly laugh in response.

"Amen," Uncle J.C. and a few other deacons rumble from the back of the sanctuary, to quiet the crowd.

Again, the preacher flicks his hand in my direction. The wet cuff of his white robe makes the preacher appear to lumber under the weight. The liquid escapes the large armhole with a waterfall sound, as the holy drops plummet back into the baptismal tub. I lower myself another step. The water above my knee, I shiver from the cold. The robe expands and sinks as the water climbs up the cloth.

The preacher reaches out and grabs my hand. He pulls me down into the tub, almost slinging me across his body. The instant I am about to go under he reaches out and catches me with his other hand.

"Not yet," he says under his breath. He holds me tight so I do not move.

The preacher speaks to the congregation about deliverance and eternity. He quotes Bible verses. His voice, drowned out by the thoughts in my head, sounds like the wish-wash syllables of the teacher in the Peanuts cartoon specials. Wha—wha-wah-wah.

Is my mom smiling?

Wah-wah-wha-wah-wah.

I hope we go to Bonanza or Western Sizzlin for dinner.

Wah-wah-wha-wah.

Can they see my peter through this robe?

I turn my head to look out at the congregation. I cannot see anything because the flowers lining the front of the baptismal area are too high. The preacher's body is close to mine, which makes me uncomfortable. The fact that I do not have on underwear and no one in the congregation can see me makes me think bad things are going to happen. I do not trust him, but I do not know why. I hang on his arm, waiting to be reborn.

He is telling the story of John baptizing Jesus and how baptism by water is the only act of salvation. With submersion comes the promise of eternity. For the first time, I understand I am trying to escape myself and create something better than the world I have been given. This is my first attempt to escape my father, my mother, and the loneliness of my childhood. I want to be reborn, a new life in front of me, one without the pain and scars weighing me down. I am too young to have scars. I need a father to teach me how to grow up a proper man.

Air shoots out the neck of the satin garment as the preacher lowers me into the water, into the arms of my new Father. The water covers me, but I'm not ready. Before I grab my nose with my free arm, the water rushes up my sinuses. I flail, a spastic fool. My feet go out from underneath me. We lose our grip on one another, my top half sinks. My feet kick the surface, splashing water high in the air. He pulls me up. I choke and cough, expelling water from my nostrils and lungs. The struggle stirs frivolity through the congregation. I hear my family laughing.

POETRY BOOKS
1977

THE OTHER KIDS have already started to line up. The library erupts with a ruckus. The library is my favorite part of second grade. I am always the last one to leave. I sit at the table, fingers rubbing the words on the page as if the contours of the print were visible to my touch. The green hardback book has yellow leaves on the front cover; the tips of the corners bent, small wrinkles run along the edges of the spine. The white pages smell of rubber cement. Some are stuck together by orange juice or something sticky so I pull them apart carefully so as to not rip the pages. I've never read a book like this one.

For the first time, I notice the format of the text. The book not divided into chapters, rather by sections. Each section titled for a season of the year. Inside each section are subsections. These pertain to months or holidays situated inside that month or season. Each subsection includes several poems; long poems that take up a page, short poems, others have only a couple of lines. The words appear free on the pages. Some of the poems take the shape of the subject, like a pumpkin, the moon, or a tree.

Something entrances me about the sentences, and the short rhyming four-line stanzas flow together with a beautiful sound as I read aloud. I understand the meanings and get a more complete picture of the story when I speak the words as I read them. I like the way the consonants and vowels blend together and roll off my tongue. The short pieces remind me of Bible verses, yet in a language I comprehend.

"Let's go, Jason," the teacher says.

I have never read poetry. I found this book by chance, sitting on a cart in front of the librarian's desk. The last thirty minutes blur. I am lost in excitement, a feeling runs through my body I do not understand. This book makes me feel alive. I now want to write poems.

"You missed the checkout time, put the book down. Get in the back of the line," she says.

I will not.

One of the boys pushes another. As soon as she turns her back, I stuff the book into my bag. Adrenaline rushes through me. My first two attempts at thievery—a Milky Way at El Fenix, and a pack of Juicy Fruit at Sadler's—I was not successful.

I want this book.

I study the faces of my classmates; none are looking at me. The librarian is not at her desk. The line of students files out past the teacher holding the door, eyes down the hall. I wait patiently next to my chair, book bag in my left hand. I do not think I am stealing the book. I tell myself I will return the copy in a few days.

I can't wait to get home and read it.

WE GATHER ON SUNDAYS
1978

WE GATHER ON SUNDAYS in a small white-framed house. My great-grandparents, Mamaw and Papaw, improved their home over the years. Time overran their poverty with technological advances like central heat and air, a dishwasher, and a washing machine. These were unaffordable luxuries for my great-grandmother for many years, but hard work kept a faithful home and Mamaw never fractured.

Every effort she's made in her life was from scratch. Ernest Morrison, my great-grandfather, shows his emotions only when it comes to my great-grandmother, Bill. She earned the nickname Bill as a child; the townsfolk knew her by her rough-and-tough exterior. Since the age of twenty, she has snorted only the finest French snuff, which she spits into a rusted Maxwell House coffee can.

The house holds four rooms, square and simple in construction. Every surface smells of Alzheimer's and bacon fat. Bill grew old by fits of forgetfulness. The thin, ancient windowpanes bubble out in the heat and bow inward from the cold: they always portray a blemished reflection. Cobweb ghost towns hang in the deep corners of bedroom ceilings. These all remind me that old people live here—folks too tired to maintain appearances. Three-step concrete stoops descend from the front and the back doors, surrounded by honeysuckle bushes. The stoops double as lounge chairs for lazy-day conversations and shelves for perspiring glasses of sweet-tea lemonade when the men play horseshoes on the lawn. It is safe here.

By the time the family caravans out of the West Glen Baptist Church parking lot and down Ferguson Road, taking a right at the Piggly Wiggly onto Lakeland Drive, my great-grandmother is already at the house finishing Sunday supper. No one misses Sunday supper.

As the six-car parade travels down Lakeland, the large hill of the railroad crossing bends the road. It resembles a ramp Evel Knievel might launch off, over a tank of surefire death. My cousin Craig, age eight and a half, and I, age seven, hold our breath in the backseat as we pantomime rocket car explosions to our doom. He the youngest grandchild, I the oldest great-grandchild, we built our bond in the backyard and at Papaw's sides at the table on Sundays. The cars pass Daytona, Diceman, and San Fernando Way. We slow for the downward dip of the turn onto Santa Clara.

The street is lush with vegetation, big pecan and oak trees create a canopy overhead. Front yards with junk-pile litter make the manicured lawns of Papaw and his immediate neighbors seem out of sorts among the uneven blocks of sidewalk, upended by roots strangled for space between the road and the walkway. Modest is an exaggeration for this home's splendor. We pull into a driveway made of grass and two tire-track strips of stone.

"Y'all hurry! Supper is on the table!" Mamaw waves from the front door, the screen resting across her large bosom.

"Jase, come on now, son, help your grandma," Papaw beckons from the porch. All of my aunts, uncles, and cousins scurry into the house for a good seat. Until I am fourteen, I never hear a sound other than laughter here.

"Heavenly Father . . ." Papaw's prayer begins. There is seriousness in the humble language he uses, as if every breath carries fatal consequence. "Bless this home and those gathered in it. Thank You for the gifts that You have given us, the richness You have brought to us, the joy that lives inside us, and forgive us our shortcomings." His prayers always end with mercy and grace for others. His God is a god of resurrection and Ernest knows about resurrection; he was born again, maybe more than once.

He eats hunched over his plate. The sideways dangle of the fork scooped with the fever of a boy who never knew if there was going to be another bite; each hurried shovel reveals a life of worry. Craig and I giggle. We kick each other's legs under the table. Mamaw reaches out and pinches the back of my left arm. Her nails, filed arrowheads, clinch the smallest amount of flesh to cause the largest amount of pain. The thin and yellowed nail bites like a sharp knife across my finger.

"Hey!" I respond, surprised by the lightning quickness of that old woman.

Craig sticks out his tongue and grins. I swear she drew blood.

Papaw swirls his sweet tea with vigor; his lips smack. "Now that is good cooking, Momma." He savors the littlest things. A small Tupperware container with a red lid sits on his right. Even when tightly closed, a pungent smell seeps out. The tattoo named *Trixie* on Papaw's right arm twists and dances away from the large purple onion he removes from it and grasps like an apple. Onions remind him of his days as an Arkansas sharecropper during the Great Depression. His smile grows larger as he devours the bitter fruit. Bill grew onions in their garden during the Depression to feed the kids and sell to other families. Ernest found them to be born of love, not labor like the rice fields. While Bill grew onions and greens, Ernest farmed rice on another man's land. But he never eats rice. Superman is not as tough as Papaw.

"You boys look like prizefighters," he says. "Never fight amongst yourselves."

"You and your brothers ever fight?" Bill interjects, knowing the answer and the story already.

"Amen, buckshot!" Uncle J.C., the second youngest of Papaw's four brothers, sings out from the living room. A buzz of laughter rises up, as everyone knows what he means.

"Tell the story about the snakes!" one of my cousins yells, followed by a chorus of agreement from the rest of the family. Bill blushes. I have never heard that story.

"Jase, we lived in Brinkley, Arkansas, during the Depression when your grandma was just a girl; took whatever job we could." Family members crowd the entry that separates the living and dining rooms. "A dollar a day: sunup, sundown." Papaw's eyes fall on what is left of the onion.

"I hate onions!" J.C. injects. "Darn things kept me skinny."

"We got to eat most days back then because she grew that garden," Aunt Irene gets the story back on track. "And you don't have to eat them anymore. Let your brother talk." She pokes at his head, so her words will make it through his receding hairline.

"We all helped each other," Papaw resumes. "Know what you're fighting for, boys." Pride overcame the scars of his poverty, sliced and burned onto his enormous hands, the kind of experience that does not come from formal education and books. Each crisp snap of his jaw against the thin layers of purple flesh holds my attention. Between each chew, I never miss his words.

"Brinkley was hot in the spring. When we got on, the owner told us there was a house down at the creek edge we could live in as long as I worked the land. Fix her up, she was ours."

"Damn house was in the water," my grandmother speaks from the kitchen entry.

"It was a four-room shotgun house; it sat on a marsh at the side of this creek. The place needed a cleaning," Papaw says.

"It needed a new everything," Mamaw mumbles through her food. "Waist-high grass; had to pull our truck loaded with all our furniture in with a tractor. My sister and I even burnt down the outhouse just to get a new one." She cracks a wicked smile.

"We had to get rid of all kinds of critters. Ate a lot of squirrels. But mainly it was the snakes," he says in eerie tones. I am terrified of snakes. "My brothers and I went hunting in the yard the day we moved in. Kids propped up on the truck to watch the show."

"You mean the disaster," J.C. foreshadows.

"Well, if you had been more careful . . ." Irene shuts him down.

"It was a sight, five grown men walking through the yard, shooting the ground. We were doing well—one snake, then three snakes, seven. Pretty quick we moved to the large side of the house connected to the back, should have had it done by lunch, we thought." Papaw smirks. "Then one bit Virgil on the boot; we all looked down and found more moccasins than earth." He pauses for a drink of tea. "All hell broke loose. Rifles shooting wildly as we bumped into, knocked down, and pushed each other out of the way. We used the butts of our guns to swat the slithering mess—there were millions—stomping, jumping, and crushing what we could. We sounded like a bunch of women as we fled the side of the house." Papaw laughs and touches Craig on the arm.

"Tell them what the brave men did next," Irene suggests with a giggle.

"Well, boys, we blamed each other. Then took to fighting as our wives watched," Papaw says. "Without so much as a word, Momma grabbed her hoe and charged right toward us." He starts to chuckle. "That is what stopped us; use to say it was the sight of determination in Bill's face. We thought she was coming for us."

Everyone laughs and Mamaw rolls her eyes. "I should have."

"We could barely see her in the high grass," J.C. adds.

"We tracked her by the metal head of the hoe as she raised it overhead. She was a banshee, never heard so much vicious killing." Papaw looks at her with a smile. She says nothing.

"The big rowdy Morrison brothers stood there with jaws hanging; little old Bill, the butcher of Brinkley, Arkansas, saving them all from the moccasins," Irene completes the picture.

"Took her a half hour to kill about ninety snakes," Papaw's tone rises with nostalgia. "Only a few weeks to eat them all." He pauses, shifting his gaze to Bill. "Only so many ways a man can eat a snake."

"Amen. Hallelujah. Amen. Fried with onions." Uncle J.C. is acting like the deacons in the back of the church. During the sermon, they shout out praise to evoke the spirit of the Holy Ghost and wake the bored sleepers that teeter in the pews.

From the broken laughter in the living room, you could tell Aunt Irene had poked her husband into shutting up.

"You got to know what is important. Family and Jesus, take care of your mommas." Papaw raises the onion in his hand at Craig and me, gives us both a smile and a look of conviction.

"Daddy, leave those boys alone," Craig's mother Annie says as she goes to refill her plate.

Papaw takes a slice of white bread and sops up the leftover gravy on his plate and the few black-eyed peas straggling at the edges. No one ever leaves food on the table. Bill is an outstanding cook who always makes the same meal on Sundays: pan-fried steaks, pan gravy, corn bread, black-eyed peas, mashed potatoes, cream-style honey corn, and Papaw's onion. The only surprise is dessert. Nine times out of ten, it's pie. Today it is pecan, made of nuts gathered from the front and backyards. Our family spent decades sitting around this table shelling those nuts, sharing stories, and weaving our family mythology. It is Ernest's favorite pie and conversation.

"Wait for the coffee, you boys," Bill gurgles, her mouth half full of corn bread. She is wider than tall, short arms and swelled legs; she wears muumuus and house shoes except on Sundays. "Y'all settle down, let me finish or go out back and pick you one."

The snap of her steely green-gray eyes is serious. She peers out over the top of the bifocals always resting midnose. We know exactly what she means. The bush off the back porch provides switches, long thick stems that thin out into delicate whips. She makes everyone pick and ready his or her own switch. We hustle back to our seats and wait.

"You learn early about Mamaw's switches, even snakes won't mess with her," my mother's sister, Barbra, chuckles to the nods of everyone else.

"Amen," chimes Aunt Irene. "Who's ready for pie?" She places her arm on my shoulder as she passes by.

The younger women gather all the supper plates and each has a specific job. Irene and my grandmother cram into the kitchen to slice the pie and pour the coffee. Bill sits at the table, empty plate in front of her, staring out the window, holding onto what yesterdays she has left. The older she becomes, the more the stories center on her. We make every effort to keep her connected to us. All the men receive coffee and pie first. Then Craig and I get ours. Every time Irene brings me my dessert, she asks the same questions.

"You know who I am? You know my name?" Her sweet smile and gray-heavy, hair-sprayed beehive hairdo hold my dessert prisoner until I tell her.

"Did *you* forget who you are?" I say with a puzzled look. "Aunt Irene."

"Bless your heart, adorable. Extra big piece for you," she clamors with a pinch to the back of my arm. "Jason, you got those traveling-salesman eyes."

"Never mind whose daddy you look like," Ernest whispers to me while the women's chatter turns to gossip at the other end of the six-chair dining room table. "You will find the truth. You're gonna be a prizefighter, boy, the reward will come when you decide to seek it." Ernest draws truth from his own life, even though I have no idea what his words mean. "You boys belong to this family; we will be in heaven together." I never heard a statement hold more truth within me. A sliver of pie in his left hand and tea in his right, he pushes back from the dining room and gets up to join the men at the card table for a game of Pitch.

"We fed those kids, Momma. All day in those rice fields; we fed those kids," Bill murmurs with a tranquil smile. Their eyes connect in a way that makes me forever jealous. Their love is the love I have sought my whole life. Time cannot contain them.

I PEER OVER THE BALCONY RAILING of the hotel suite with a bottle of whiskey in one hand and a cell phone in the other. Dallas spreads out eight floors beneath me.

I fantasize about jumping, dreaming big. My torso stretches over the railing, arms extended with a gaudy *fuck you* flying off both my hands. The insane flaps of my appendages as I fall. I am naked.

The ultimate belly flop.

Although in my case, more like a devastating thud of dehydrated skin and bones. There would be an aftermath, the chill of the investigators trying to discover how the walls of this room consumed me.

The past four days are a blur. I became conscious a half hour ago, in a pool of my own vomit, hovering above my clothes sticking out of my duffel bag.

Four days.

Given my present circumstances, leaping out into the darkness seems like a logical, Hollywood conclusion.

I should put on underwear, just in case.

The sliding glass door is open. I reject this obvious act of cowardice and step back inside.

I dial my grandmother's number. Cold spring morning fills the hotel room. The other line rings for the fourth, fifth, sixth time. I can't stop shaking, pacing the room.

She answers.

"You awake?" I say.

"Jason, is that you? Where are you?"

I hesitate, the silence on the phone line crackles. My grandmother clears her throat. I know she is startled. She always saves me. Her downfall is that she loves to help other people even when they use her.

"You doing all right?" I ask. "Hope you've been okay."

"Jason Carney, where are you calling me from?" she snaps. "Caller ID says the Embassy Suites—which one?"

"Off I-35," I say. "I really fucked up."

There is panic in my voice. I honestly want her help. Scared of my own death, I no longer have patience for my all-consuming fear. My chest hurts. My life is the constant repetition of something burning placed to my lips.

What has happened to me?

"We know you have, honey. All kinds of folks are looking for you. Somebody called, said you were supposed to have some shows in New York that you missed, your man from Global Talent is looking for you too."

"I need you to pick me up in the morning and take me to rehab."

"Oh Jason, how bad is it?" she says. "What time do you want me to come, Jase?"

"Seven."

"I will be there. Might be late because of rush hour. You're on the other side of the city, but I will be there."

"Promise?"

"Promise," she says. "Don't go anywhere. Do you hear me? Don't go anywhere."

"I am going to sleep. Thank you, Grandma."

I tell her the room number and that I love her. We hang up.

For the first time in a month, I feel like I am turning a corner, going home. A home I no longer have, smoked away with truth. The greater truth being that I am out of dope. This addiction leads me to the truth of my own death; a death I fear. I also fear being out of crack. My blue metal pipe floats in the bottom of the toilet. Sweat rolls down my back. I tingle and pulse. I want to believe I am going to sleep. The pipe is still in there. The bowl is fresh. Only one tug before the toilet flushes. I imagine myself cleaning the tube and getting a large hit.

I am stupid for trying to flush it.

My cell phone beeps, C is sending me a text message: *You about ready?*

I am paranoid that he and his friends are watching me. He is too accurate at knowing when I am out and in need of more.

I should have told her that in case they come in and kidnap me.

Now thoughts of C race through my head. I walk into the bathroom. My muscles ache. I do not want to leave. My mind spins.

I need to get some more.

The reality of what is happening sets in. No more high. Sobriety starts now. I look into the toilet. The edge of the crushed blue tube peeks out of the bottom of the bowl.

One hit to calm my mind.

The water runs from the ends as I lift the stem out of the toilet. The blue metal squashed by my heel cradles what remains of the dope melted on the chore. I press the tube into a towel. The water dances out of the end. The hair dryer on the wall comes to life in a flick of the switch. Water shoots out the end as the heat fills the tube. I rotate the ends. Each gets a turn under the heat.

The process takes a couple of minutes. I am careful not to spend too much time glaring at my reflection. Unwashed for days, I cannot remember my last hour of true sleep. The pipe is the focus. The lighter erupts.

The chore inside the tube sizzles with moisture. The smoke tastes foul. The effect of the dope is the same. My body eases with euphoria, even before I exhale. I sit on the toilet, my whole body unknotting.

I need more.

Three simple words roll across my mind and all the resolve of the phone conversation disintegrates. I no longer think of my grandmother, escaping back to life. Instead, I could be at the crack house in thirty minutes, back at the hotel in an hour.

Could easily sit and smoke until Freeda arrives.

I decide to go replenish my stash, smoke until morning.

Then I will quit.

CARNATIONS
1978

THE LOBBY IN BAYLOR MEDICAL CENTER smells of cleaning fluid, a scent of fear that burns in my nostrils. A sterile silence covers every surface with the feeling of impending death. All of the workers, patients, and visitors amble across the floor ignoring the hideous air, as if the stench was normal.

My mom will not be coming back.

I understand that I interrupted her life because single teenage mothers do not get to go to college and they have a hard time finding a man. I blame myself for my father leaving, for her headaches, and the dreamless life she finds herself living.

I sit in one of two identical chairs across from the elevators while my grandmother waits for the doors to open. Orange vinyl sticks like plastic wrap to my leg.

I do not want to be here.

My grandmother turns and smiles at me with the ding of the elevator arriving. She says, "You sit over here. I'll be right back. Then we'll go up and you can visit with your mom. She really misses you."

I do not believe her.

If she misses me so much, why have I been at Craig's house for one month?

Alone, I study my surroundings. A pretty woman sits at the information desk near the front, working her shiny hair more than the phone lines. A couch and two chairs, separated by a coffee table on top of a large brown abstract rug, seem out of place in the middle of the floor across from the desk and the lazy woman with a hard-working brush. The ensemble appears to be right out of a furniture store window. Even the lamps on the end table have cords dangling off the sides tied in loops, not plugged into anything.

They just want you to think everything is normal. This is not a place I want to feel comfortable.

Beyond the far lamp is the gift shop, more of a drugstore. They sell sodas, snacks, greeting cards, medications, and flowers.

I should buy some flowers for my mom.

I check my pants pockets: two quarters, three pennies, and a dime. I am not buying much. I cross the floor, walking as if I belong here. I strut like John Travolta carrying two cans of paint down a crowded sidewalk in the only scene from the movie *Saturday Night Fever* I can recall. The music in my head bounces out of my legs, the perfect song for this place. Lost in my own world, I must look ridiculous.

Mom loves the Bee Gees.

The store is pristine. All the products line the shelves without empty spaces; the cleanliness suggests someone has a lot of time on their hands. The labels face the front, standing at attention. The old man behind the pharmacy counter has a crew cut; the silver stubble reveals a mole above his left ear which sticks out above his black-frame glasses.

"You doing all right, son?" he asks with a smile.

"No, I need some flowers for my mom, please, sir."

"Dorothy!" he calls out.

An older woman emerges from behind the front counter. She wears a lavender blouse with a large silver butterfly broach clasped to a purple-speckled scarf around her neck. Her hair is stiff with hair spray. As she approaches, I smell the Aqua Net. Her smile is even more fragrant, revealing unblemished teeth between candy-apple lips. She glides over the carpet.

"What can I do for you?" she asks.

"I want to buy flowers for my mom," I say, knowing I don't have any money.

"In a vase or an arrangement in paper?"

"What's the difference?" I ask, playing dumb.

"About ten dollars."

"Then paper, please."

"What kind of flowers do you want?"

"My mom likes carnations. Red ones."

"Red carnations, how many?"

"Three. One for her past, present, and future." I am proud of myself.

"Wow," she says. "You have thought about this a little."

"Been saving my money all week," I smile. This line worked before.

She chuckles. As she wraps the flowers in the green tissue, she winks at me. "How about a red ribbon?" The question is rhetorical, as she ties the ribbon before I can answer. "How about a nice card for your mother?"

"No thank you, ma'am."

She punches the buttons on the ancient cash register. I hear the gears tumble loudly as the numbers roll to the correct amount. I prepare my insides for what will happen next.

"That'll be three dollars and seventy-six cents."

I study the contents of my hand, slowly counting each coin two or three times. I look up at her in pain. "This is all I've got," I say, handing her the change.

"Sweetie, you're about three dollars short."

I stare at her blankly, waiting. She looks confused.

"Is there anyone who . . ."

On cue, I start to cry. "I don't want my mommy to die. Can you help my mommy?"

"Sweetie, she is going to be all right. God will protect her."

"No He won't," I blubber, "He is going to take her to heaven."

I continue to rake up three dollars' worth of tears. The look on her face is anguished. She probably deals with customers visiting terminal family and friends most days. I just bet they are not eight-year-olds with convincing blue eyes sparkling with saltwater.

Surely, I am breaking her heart.

I wipe my nose and face on my arm. A long trail of snot latches to the thin pale hairs of my forearm. The string snaps, flings onto my shirt. I smear the snot with my hand for effect. Her face crinkles with compassion and disgust.

"You poor thing. Here, take the flowers." She hands me the flowers and a napkin. "Wipe your eyes; your mommy is going to love the flowers. You go on now, God bless."

"Thank you." *That was not so hard.* "God bless you too."

PINK ROBES
1978

I SQUEEZE MY GRANDMOTHER'S HAND, unsure of what to expect. Three carnations in my left hand, I ask my grandmother, "Do you think she will like the flowers?"

"Yes, sweetie, she will. Aren't you just full of surprises, saving your lunch money all week? Now, remember to tell your mom that she looks pretty. She really misses you."

The elevator doors open into a large corridor. Directly across is a large window wall that runs the length of the hallway off to the right. At the end of it is a large security checkpoint with a set of sliding glass doors.

There is no privacy here.

I can see people in robes and hospital gowns on the other side of the glass.

It is like being at the zoo.

All of the people look disoriented. Few appear to have taken a bath or combed their hair. Hygiene does not seem to be important on the other side of the glass.

I want to go back downstairs.

Those gathered around the tables play cards. Their heavy faces do not smile as they fumble through the motions. Others sit in chairs smoking. They watch the television perched in a box on the wall, while a few amble about the large open room, staring off into space. Behind this communal area, a row of doors open into bedrooms. Over in the corner stands a woman with blond hair, in a light pink robe, her back to us. She teeters back and forth. My skin crawls.

She looks like my mom. I hope that is not her.

The strands of her hair spindle out, rigid wisps float in the air. Each strand is frail and translucent against the light, matted in such a way that she appears to be balding; but that is just an illusion.

She is too short to be my mom.

"She is so excited you're here," my grandmother says.

"Me too." I cannot take my eyes off the large glass-enclosed room.

Why are they locked in there? They must be contagious. What is that woman doing?

I understand the term *suicide*, but this is my first encounter with mental illness. The horror of this place lurks in the silence of the hallway. Our shoes stick to the linoleum, each stride like the sound of adhesive peeling back. Walking down the hallway, I can see over the shoulder of the woman in the pink robe. She stares into the mirror, applying lipstick. I do not see the lipstick canister. Her vanity allows her to pretend. I begin to consider my own appearance.

I should have cleaned up for Mom.

"We cannot stay long; you're not old enough to be up here," my grandmother explains. "The doctor is going to let her visit for ten minutes."

"Okay," I mutter, wondering what kinds of people bring kids to the crazy house. "Why is this glass wall here?"

"People on this floor have to be locked up," she replies.

"Why?"

"Because they may be a danger to themselves or others." She hesitates, shaking her head, rethinking her last statement. "Your mom is doing fine, she's just a little tired with all the headaches."

They don't lock you up for headaches.

I PULL INTO THE APARTMENTS. I am on a mission. I scan the gate. C is nowhere around.

Damnit, he is supposed to meet me at the gate.

A lookout recognizes me, punches in the access code to enter. I drive slowly into the maze of buildings. At night, this apartment complex is a different world. From dusk to midnight, dealers and hustlers sit on their porches and cars, waiting for the drive-through drug-and-flesh sales to begin. They do not like strangers around here. If you do not know someone, the dealers will not sell to you. Half the cars rolling through are strangers. Easy to spot, they sit outside the gate waiting for another car to roll up and let them inside the mall. All regular customers give the access code. Once inside, it is up to the dealer to keep the customers faithful. I know the code. I only talk to and buy from C.

A commotion breaks out between two parked cars, off to my right. I slow to see what's up. Two figures, a man and woman, argue. She appears to be older than he is, by years. She looks tough, street worn. Her clothes hug the contours of her large belly, sticking out from under her shirt. Her gray shorts scream that no woman this big fits in shorts so small. She wears house shoes. I judge her to be an out-of-work streetwalker.

His hands are around her throat. Her hands are in the air in surrender. I stop, unsure if I should get involved. I watch. He slaps her. He raises his head and I clearly see his face. I recognize C. He slaps her again. He yells at her between his clenched teeth, the veins in his neck bulge and pulse. She does not fight back. In between two parked cars, she has nowhere to run. He shoves her to the ground. Her short bleached-blond wig falls to the ground. She cries. He does not care. I do nothing. She is on her hands and knees. She tries to get off the ground. He does not let her, a swift knee to the side of her head pins her face against a car door. I hear the air escape her mouth as her body crumples. She no longer looks tough.

"Better do what I say, bitch!"

"I will! I will!" she replies, face now against the asphalt.

He kicks the backs of her legs. His feet fly over and over again, legs to midsection. She does not move.

"Better shut up, bitch, and start paying me my money!"

Her tears turn to pleas for him to stop. He does not.

"Don't tell me what to do!" he yells.

He draws his leg back, kicking her one more time. Mid-swing, he notices my car idling with the window down. Before his leg comes down, the smile of a salesperson sprouts over his face.

"Clockwork, my muthafucka," his leg comes down, "you look a little freaked out! How the hell you doing?"

"Please stop! Please! Please, I'll do better," she cries.

He steps over her and spits onto her back. His fangs retract. The hustle of our fake friendship consumes him. She does not get up. She waits for him to finish correcting her. I don't know how to react. I just know I never want to be on the ground with him over me.

"J, what up, my brother?" he says, climbing into the passenger seat. "Take me to Burger King and the house. My day is about over."

"Who's that?" I ask.

"Some stupid bitch that better get me my money!" he

screams out the window in her direction as I turn the car around. "How much you need?"

GUNS AND MAIL SLOTS
1974

"DON'T LET HIM IN, DEBBIE!" My mom's best friend Pam is frantic from a loud banging on the front door.

Awakened by the commotion, I stand at the dark top of the stairwell looking down on the entryway. The angle of the stairs seems steep to me and a long way to the bottom. The pounding continues. The vibrations flow along the closed curtains of the living room window. Unable to comprehend the weight of Pam's panic, I hide in the shadows, confused and frightened.

"He just wants to talk," my mom says.

"Don't be stupid! Sit down and be quiet," Pam says. The violence of the pounding increases.

My mother and Pam are invisible, far back in the living room, only their voices identifying their locations. I stand mute and motionless.

"Open the fucking door and talk to me!"

The slams on the bolted door rattle the brass plates covering the mail slot every time his fists hit it. I feel feeble. A warm sensation runs down my leg, settling in the padded bottoms of my footy pajamas. I stand there, wet and breathless.

"Why are you doing this to me? I love you!"

"Go away, Roy!" Pam screams.

Pam, much smaller than my mother, wears a curly perm and has a toughness my mother lacks. Pam came over after my mother called her earlier in the evening. Roy spent the afternoon drinking and belittling my mother for her house-cleaning abilities. They fought. Disgusted, he left in his company work van. Pam's strong sense of family had given my father the benefit of the doubt for the last time. In case he returned, she took us to dinner.

"This needs to be the end, Debbie. Think of Jason," she says to my mother as we eat Mexican food. "He will kill you both one day."

"I know. I know," my mother says.

She picks at her food nonchalantly, as if she does not believe it. I do not understand his anger. I see it but I do not think it is real. I place it deep within me near imaginary friends who can suppress its pain. They hold me in their arms when black-eye midnights rip me from my bed.

"Nothing has changed. He's still an asshole," Pam says.

"I want him to go. I can't make him leave." My mother starts to cry. "What has happened to me? I love him so much."

"His love is sick, Debbie. How many beatings do you need?" Pam holds her hand. "We can do it tonight."

"Okay."

We return home. My dad gone, they gather his things.

Now, a chill runs over my arms and legs. The impacts cease. An electric hum races over the air, then a few moments of surreal silence. I hear the heavy breath of the women downstairs. Each inhale, a frightened question. "Did he go away?"

"Come on, Deb, let me in." My daddy's voice sounds calm and ordinary. "We need to work things out."

"Go away, Roy," Pam says, "y'all can talk tomorrow."

"Stay out of this, Pam! Please let me talk with my wife."

The round bottoms of his fists knock on the door again as he leans against it.

"Open the door, bitch! This is my house!" Roy's rage flows like the discipline of a sprinter, who exerts his will in quick bursts containing immense power. "This is my fucking house!"

I want to go to the door, to quiet the storm. Trapped between two parents and a situation I do not understand, my pretend friends hold me in place. I want to order my parents to love each other. We loved each other—pieced together puzzles, played records, took pictures, and made his lunch together. I do not understand why complicated adults mess up good things.

My mother, still not convinced that ignoring him is the best policy, comes to the door. She does not see me hidden in the darkness of the stairwell. I make myself rigid, not wanting to get in trouble. Pam holds her ground on the other side of the room.

"Debbie, if you don't open that door, don't ever call me again," my dad says.

My mom stands motionless, the palms of her hands resting on the door. Confusion surrounds her. Bewildered at the upside-down nature of her daily life, my mom hesitates.

"He's crazy, Debbie," Pam pleads.

"You fucking bitch!" My dad starts kicking the door.

My mother jumps back, terrified; she knows what is coming.

"I'm gonna kill you, bitch, you fucking whore! This is my fucking house! Don't laugh at me, you bitches—fucking dykes!" he screams, lost in another reality.

He hurls his whole body against the blocked entrance; it sounds like a bomb. I love him, even though sometimes I do not want to. She needs to unlock the door.

"I've got my gun, Roy! You hear me? I got my gun!" Pam screams at the door, pulling my mother back out of my sight. "You hear me, Roy?"

The minutes pass in silence. Pam and my mother both jump when the phone rings. The conversation is distraught and abrupt.

"What, Roy? She doesn't want to talk." Pam remains stern. "Don't come back here. I have my gun! Roy, I will call the police . . . Yes, I'm sure I have the gun . . . Who are you calling a lying bitch? . . . What do you mean, you broke into my house? Roy, don't be stupid, I have my gun . . . I am calling the police, don't come back here!"

She hangs up the phone in a frenzy.

"We have to go," she tells my mom. I hear fast shuffling as Pam gathers her things. She drops her keys as she picks up her purse, which empties out when she bends over for the keys. "Goddamnit, come on, Debbie, let's go!"

"Why? What did he say?"

"He broke into my house and stole my gun!" she yells, throwing her valuables back into her black leather bag.

"He doesn't have your gun. *You* have your gun," my mother says. I stand in the stairwell waiting for my mom to discover me there, wet and crying.

"I don't have my gun, I left it at home. I don't want to find out how he knew that."

The door almost caves in from the thunderous impact of the human cannonball that then roars across the parking lot. Both women downstairs lurch with fright. Our only family photograph rattles off the wall between the front door and the living room window. Thin glass crashes into jagged shards all over the linoleum entryway.

"Let me in this fucking house! I want to talk with you!" my father shouts. "Open this fucking door!"

"Call the police! Call the damn police!" Pam cries out.

"Fuck you, Roy, you bastard!" my mother yells.

Light-headed, unsure of what to think about the violence of the shaking door, I stare at the mail slot. I want to crawl inside that space, because I connect my parents. They have to listen to me. It is my duty to intervene. My daddy on the other side of the door, he wants to come home. I do not understand why Mommy doesn't want to talk with him. He loves us. I need to unlock it.

"Go away, Roy! Why are you doing this?" my mom wails.

I start down the stairs. A triumphant feeling, my solution: if we just talk about the good things, the bad would not seem so bad anymore. I look back up the stairs. My invisible friends give me courage and protection. It is too late to change my mind. I stand directly in front of my fear, covered in piss.

"Open the door! I hear you standing there!" he yells in unison with his blows.

The hairs stand up on the back of my neck.

"I hear you, bitch! Open the door! I got something for you cunts!"

My mind keeps screaming, Stop, Daddy, stop!

I cannot force the sound out of my frozen mouth. The chain out of my reach, it jumps along the track securing it to the door. The hinges are coming off. He will crush me under its weight, laughing at the bloody pool of my pain.

I remember us swimming the previous summer, alone in the apartment complex's pool. The afternoon sun fell behind the tree line while we bathed in the cool wind of the shade. I laughed as he pulled me around the water. Roy was gigantic to me. His hands grasped and towed the red flotation ring I sat inside, unable to swim. He stood shoulder-deep as he pushed me out over the water, never letting me float away too long.

The last time he sent me out laughing with safety, he pulled my legs as the ring sailed back. I slipped through. Under the water, I choked and sank. He chuckled with a muted grin. I woke up on the side of the pool, my father giving me mouth-to-mouth.

"I got something for you! You will not disrespect me!"

His voice now hovers through the hinged bends of the mail slot. "I got something to show you, Deb!"

"Daddy," I say to the covering. Time slows to a quarter of its natural speed, I put my face right up to the opening.

My father's hand shoves through the slot. The short black metal barrel rams against the bridge of my nose. Blood surges from my nostrils. I scream as I stare at the gun. My father's face resembles a frustrated clown, both insane and happy. He does not remove his hand or the gun.

"Let Daddy in, he's not going to hurt you or Mommy. Let Daddy in, Daddy is only joking with Mommy."

"Get away from the door, Jason!" my mommy yells, yanking me back. The lid of the mail slot makes a muffled ding as it lands on the barrel of the handgun.

I will never feel safe with him again.

Riddle

We forget ourselves whole among the holy.
Murmur illusions from the organs of our sex.

Laughter and lust flicker like wasps
tongue upon tongue, a vespine dance.

Disguise our bodies in bitter bouquets.
We fracture. Use our bones to plumb

the depths of each other's scars. We grind
salt in between our teeth—nuzzle forever

at our lips. The flower of your eye tears
like communion behind brown hair. You

bellow as a puncture wound. Our fingers stain.
Our love evokes the crimson throat of the son.

FIRST JOB
1981

"I HATE BABYSITTING," I SAY.

Every morning starts too early for an eleven-year-old on summer vacation. Awake and out the door before the sun is up, I return home most evenings around nine.

"I don't care. You keep your commitments," my mom says.

She volunteered me for the job three weeks earlier. Debbie met a couple at the pool; they have two children—a boy eight and a girl two. As she reached into the cooler for another cold one, my mother oversold my skill set as a latchkey only child who knows how to make dinner without burning down the house. Bad choices for important decisions always go down better with a buzz.

"Jason is really excellent with children, mature for his age," she told them. Debbie likes to talk out her ass after she's killed a few.

I have tread water for twenty-seven days. The twenty-eighth day should be my last. I fear drowning.

"I want to have fun. It's summer," I plead. "I want to go visit Dad."

"Goddamnit, boy, don't be so fucking selfish! Now, get your ass ready." Her last words on the subject ignore the brittle despair in my voice. I am in over my head. "Don't forget to make your lunch. Load the dishwasher before you go," she says, shutting the front door.

Babysitting is a high school girl's job. I still have to go spend the night with my grandmother when my mom goes out on the weekend. I want to go swimming.

Each thought anchors deep animosity, the weight of which slows my legs. My blue Mongoose bike crawls past the townhome community pool, as a light mist levitates above the grass. Everything is surrounded by the cloudless sky in a humid purple swelter of morning.

"You're late," the woman scolds me, as if I was her child. "Today, do a better job on the kitchen." She scurries about the living room inspecting everything; her focus is putting on her earrings. "Don't forget to vacuum and dust. Where's your lunch?" she asks, grabbing her purse. "Hun, let's go! Jason, don't eat all my food." She does not even look at us as she leaves the door half-open behind her.

"All right, little man," her husband says.

He brushes the milk off his mustache; the thick, coarse brown hairs remind me of Magnum PI. All he ever offers me is criticism. *Don't eat my snacks; clean the kitchen better; don't complain, this job is easy.*

"Have fun today, buddy," he says. Seated at the table with his son, he reaches out and strokes him on the head. As he stands, he leans over to kiss him. The boy smiles back, tickled by the texture of his father's upper lip.

Something inside me cringes. My insides course in two directions. I crave a father's attention, strokes on the head at breakfast that would fill me with confidence and aspirations, someone to teach me about mustaches and aftershave. I imagine secret manhood rituals take place standing over a sink, where fathers and sons exchange riddles of the universe. Two reflections meld to one in a fogged-up mirror. The father and son at the table give off the pungent scent of adoration. It smells of red tackle boxes full of lures and stink bait, the guts of a catfish squished in your palm, peanuts and soda at thirty-five thousand feet. All the things I do alone. I despise this whiff.

The man and woman exit to their workdays without offering a thank you, goodbye, or an estimated time of return.

"There's a note for you," the little boy says.

He is thin, practically half my size. He hides his face behind brown hair; it dangles into his cereal bowl. He hates me about as much as I hate being here. We never play together. Most days he is out the door by nine, I do not see him until lunch at three or four. Then he is gone again. His summer is an abundant imagination raw and at full tide.

His friends gather at the creek to fish. They jump their bikes along the climbs and dips of the dirt trail. They sweat and build grime under their nails, howling like animals running the wooded trails of the creek. Bottle-rocket bicycle, chicken fights, watching fourteen-year-olds shoot fireworks at one another; they compare scorched clothes and burnt skin with explosive laughter. The younger kids school together on the sides like fish, educate themselves by gazing mesmerized at the remains of the launched projectiles. They race their bikes through the small U-shaped streets of the complex, calling each other names, *douche bag, pussy lips, ball sack*. They express their freedom by mimicking the older boys. They splash the daylight from the pool, late in the afternoon, when the concrete has absorbed the sun's heat. At night, the concrete regurgitates the full contents of its belly. The heat cascades up through the darkness back toward the stars. The boys return home exhausted. They live the summer of my dreams.

I do his chores, his parents' chores, and the little girl's, five days a week. I hate it. Last night's dinner dishes pile in the sink, clean laundry in baskets ready for me to fold. I'm overworked and underpaid; his parents shorted me twenty dollars each of the first two weeks. The first time, I ate too much. The second time, I apparently did not clean enough. They never come home on time. I babysit through their happy-hour indulgences. Last Friday night they arrived at midnight, drunk, without any money left to pay me. Dirty dishes, soiled clothes, drunken adults, and dirty diapers: I hate the parents as much as I hate the boy.

As I look at the handwritten letter, the large hurried swoosh of the ink scrawls create visuals in my mind. This woman whose streaked-blond Farrah Fawcett hairdo—each strand hair-sprayed to its neighbor, as if they were one cohesive, paralyzed body and all five years out of date—bounced in a unified resentment as she wrote. My eyes roll as I read.

Do a better job cleaning! My daughter, she now has a rash. Also, do not tell my son what to do. He has permission to play with his friends and monitor himself. You boys are too close in age for one to rule over the other. Do not tell him to clean up. You are the one paid to babysit.

"Why don't you babysit, then?" I ask him.

"I'm not old enough," he smirks, getting up from the table. The boy prances upstairs, leaving his mess on the table for me.

The little girl wakes up at eight in the morning. Her room is perfect. The walls covered in brightly colored pictures of angel-winged teddy bears, flowers, and white fluffy clouds embracing rainbows. The crib lined in white lace bedding with pink swirls matches the cushions of the rocking chair angled into the corner next to it. This room is safe and full of love, creating a carbuncle of jealousy under my skin. I imagine her daddy rocking her into a giggling slumber. Every toy is clean and flawlessly arranged. I retrieve her from the crib, remove her pajamas, and begin the laborious diaper changing.

I hate this responsibility. She smiles right into my frustration, her happiness confounding me. I tolerate the discomfort, similar to the visits to my dad's house. I live all year waiting for summer, clinging to a lonely child's dream.

Maybe this year I will fly to St. Louis, be the center of my father's life, even if only for a couple of weeks.

For a few years, I did climb aboard a Boeing 737 with unlimited peanuts and sodas. I spent my days fishing at the pond on my stepmother's family's pig farm. At night, we gathered in the house my father owned with his new family. We cooked what I caught and we ate at a walnut-stained picnic table. I sat across from my dad, his gaze fixated on the smile of my little half-sister perched in his lap like a songbird. I never found my way to the black center of his eye, where I looked for some magical love evoked from his heart, a magic other than the violence-saturated memories of his first family. My sister never left his smile.

The diaper looks awkward and off-center. I fumble with the white adhesive straps across the sides. She wears only the diaper. We wait until after her nap to pick out an ensemble. I long for her nap time after lunch. Her closed eyes are the only break from my responsibilities all day. She looks like a doll, bubbling curly blond hair around bright loving blue eyes. I make her laugh with funny voices and imitations of animals.

"Moo, moo," I say, exaggerating my facial expression. "MOO!"

"Mil," she says with a smile of confidence.

She only speaks two words: *Daddy* and *milk*.

Once we come down, I secure the baby fence along the base of the stairs. We eat Cheerios and drink orange juice; she likes to stick the cereal to our faces. I enjoy the gluey wet fuss of her hands decorating my cheeks. We spend our morning watching television. *Sesame Street* turns into Bob Barker's models, selling trips to Austria with their bathing-suit smiles. She loves game shows. I love women in bathing suits.

"Come on down!" I yell as I tickle her stomach.

She giggles and tries to tickle me back. Soon, the boy bounds down the stairs carrying a toy machine gun and a backpack. A green bandanna tied around his forehead, and wearing camouflage pants and a T-shirt without sleeves, he resembles the brainwashed offspring of a backwoods militia man training for the great race war. He packs a lunch large enough for a legion of men: six sandwiches, seven little bags of chips, three apples, and a six-pack of Coke; he even empties a whole package of Oreos into his brown paper grocery sack. He loads the bag into the backpack. Rethinking his menu, he removes three cookies, placing them back into the package. I think this is curious. He leaves the package on the table, next to this morning's breakfast mess.

"I'm going to the creek to play war," he announces, slamming the door behind him.

I stare out the window into the blinding sun. He peddles into the white-hot morning, disappears around the corner. He carries my dream of freedom with him. I sit down empty.

I fold the laundry, taking my time to ensure no complaints before they pay me. The little girl plays with a floatation device she uses at the pool. A brightly colored ring, it resembles a beach ball. I had one just like it when I could not swim. She bounces her bottom off the edges, trying not to wobble onto the floor. She laughs every time she falls.

The laundry folded, piled neatly into the plastic baskets, I walk into the torture of the kitchen. The dishes unrinsed, piled all over the counters, pans crusted with pork-and-beans and fried potatoes, and the sink a jumble of cups and coffee mugs. The leftovers rotting in the trash can open my nostrils, the stink tangy upon my tongue. The mess reminds me of home and that I already cleaned a kitchen today.

Shit, this is going to take forever.

I unload the dishes I did yesterday from the dishwasher. Sunshine pours into the enclosed patio off the living area. Drawn into the comfort of the glow, my will to finish the kitchen vanishes. The deep green of the leaves gives the room a sedate feeling; the enclosed patio sparkles with tranquility. I take a break. For lunch, I plan for fish sticks and applesauce. Hungry, I grab an Oreo from the package and inhale it. A small band of black crumbs escapes out the sides of my mouth; I smear them across my cheeks with the back of my hand. The front door opens.

"Hey, sunshine." I recognize the man's voice. "I forgot my wallet." He hurdles the baby gate, taking two stairs at a time.

He descends the stairs slowly, counting the contents of his billfold. I lurk at the entry of the kitchen, wondering who he distrusts: his son, his wife, or me. He enters the kitchen nudging my shoulder with his arm. A smile across his face indicates everything in his wallet is in order.

"What the hell is this mess?" he raises his voice at the sight of the half-cleaned kitchen. "Goddamnit, Jason!" His eyes catch the empty bag of cookies. "You have to eat every fucking one of my cookies?"

"I didn't eat the cookies," I say.

"Don't lie to me, you little pig, there are crumbs all over your face. Clean this shit up. Put some fucking clothes on her."

He snags the last two Oreos as he huffs toward the front door. My frustration at being blamed for what his son did, the names adults call me, and these disheveled jackass people—their laziness, using me as a slave to scrub burnt tuna casserole off metal pans—drives the passivity from my mouth.

"Your son ate the cookies!" I scream.

"Don't yell at me, little boy," the man replies. "Blaming your theft on my son will not get you paid tonight."

He bends at the waist and picks up the girl. His determined footsteps, each an assertion of anger, conjures my father. He stomps toward the stairs. His foot comes down on the flotation ring, the seams bubble under the pressure, fissures erupt along the body of the adhesive. The detonation reverberates off the walls as the seams explode. The little girl and I bust with emotion as the halves separate from what was whole. My life changes forever.

"Cocksucker!" he screams. "Clean this shit up!"

The red fume of his face matches the color of the tulips in the center of the dining room table. His feet tangle in the flat ring, he knocks over a laundry basket. He stumbles. The clumsy way he pitches her on the couch as he falls causes her to roll off the cushion. Her head smacks the floor.

"See what you did, Jason? Pick this shit up! You are worthless!" His eyes glare like my father's, full of venom and death. "I got to get back to work."

The door slams heavy. The coatrack falls off a nail and gashes the wall. The little girl bawls. A red welt visible on her forehead, she crawls to the door, clutching after her father.

"Fuck you!" I scream tears down my face. "GGGGGGGGGRRRRRRAAAAAAAAAA!"

My guttural roar scares the girl. She claws after the doorknob just out of reach. She wants someone to hold her, ease her pain, and kiss her injured forehead, making the boo-boo better. My head swirls with rage, my reflection in the living room mirror reveals the anguish of a drowning boy. The edges of my vision blur to blackness. I tingle from head to toe, every nerve ending alive.

Who is she to feel hurt when I am the one they shit on?

"Shut up!" I scream.

"Dada. Dada. Dada!" She stretches on her tiptoes; snot and tears run down her belly.

"Shut up! Shut up! Shut up!" I yell.

"Dada! Dada!"

"He isn't coming back. Shut up!"

Our eyes connect; a hatred of everything small and fragile flows through me. I slap the back of her head with my right hand. She cries louder, and her pleas touch a place of fear within her for the first time. I recognize it in her eyes. My father showed me this anger that dwelled like a beast within my bowels. When its hideous mouth opened, I felt its infectious tongue, I found comfort within its embrace—a nightmarish life of powerless lust. I no longer fear that beast. I relish its comfort. I desire its power.

"Shut the fuck up!" I scream, slapping her head, both arms flailing in unison with my words. "They don't love you! Shut up!"

I pick her up and throw her on the couch. The red welt on her forehead the least of her pain, she quickly gets up and starts for the door. I grab her, lifting her to eye level, and shake her in my face. Her shoulders and neck jerk uncontrollably.

"Will you shut up? They're not coming!"

Her face swells with tears and her eyes jump wildly around the room, glossy and abandoned. I push her back onto the brown fake-leather cushions. Her cries morph into screams, into the fiendish prayer of innocence, an incorruptibility I no longer know. The realization of what I lack drives me over the edge.

"Shut up, shut up, shut up, shut up, shut up!"

A strange supremacy rushes through me. I cannot identify this passion. The will it gives me to choke this little girl, to silence her screams, to heal my wounds through their infection of another. I smile, sucking in the wetness from my jowls. Goose pimples erupt on my flesh, a million little fangs on my skin clamor for more. I am hungry for more control, more power, more contact with this vile lust. No thoughts direct

me. I travel a braille map of scars along my insides. I am rec-
reating a familiar horror.

I am my father's son.

S ECOND STRING
1985

"WERE THOSE BOYS MAKING FUN OF YOU?" Mom asks.

I shrug and dig my fists deeper into my pockets.

She's talking about the boys at the football banquet hours earlier. Tonight was the much-anticipated Oak Park High School letter ceremony, a potluck dinner celebrating the efforts of the small suburban football team. The ceremony and dinner were held in the fully carpeted gymnasium. Even the basketball court with its big eagle emblem is made of carpet. This small community at the edge of Agoura Hills, California, is secluded and tight knit. It's so small that the high school and junior high are on the same campus. There are only around 140 students in both schools, so everyone knows each other, has grown up together, and the majority of the people here are Jewish. No one here talks with a twang. All the parents, players, and coaches treated the barbecue brisket my mother made for the banquet as some kind of foreign delicacy, never before seen or tasted. The dish was much more popular than the bucket of Pioneer fried chicken the starting quarterback's mom brought and served.

Oak Park is the smallest place we have ever lived. We moved here with my stepfather in July from Glendale, California. It's a true hellhole for an awkward kid from Mesquite, Texas. Frankly, I think the whole state of California sucks ass—palm trees, street gangs, the ocean, smog, Disneyland, traffic, and those fucking singing raisins. I have taken many opportunities to show my disgruntled view of the current state of affairs, in ways most people would not see as positive. I never wanted to move here.

"I thought you were doing better here," my mother says. "Aren't you happy?"

Have you been paying attention?

In fact, I measure my time in this godforsaken place by the displeasure I have experienced. My first day at Herbert Hoover High School in Glendale last January, I was informed all the classes were full for the semester—I was given English, PE, science, and the same beginning typing course three times a day—SsSsSs UuUuUu CcCcCc KkKkKk.

I took typing in seventh and eighth grades. When am I ever going to need the skill of knowing how to type?

My mother once said, "A diverse skill set makes a well-rounded man." Mesquite, Texas, my home, offered what I considered diversity: Baptist, Methodist, Lutheran, and Catholic—Christian and white. Just walking through the door of Hoover and mingling with the students was an uncomfortable cultural lesson in languages, odors, and attitudes. I had never heard of countries such as Armenia and Ecuador. My biggest education came from the Philippine break dance gang; they chased me home from school to kick my ass. They wore matching sleeveless black T-shirts with a hood, a nickname, and a number on the back. The leader had a tail of hair hanging down to his ass, he would pop-and-lock punch me in the face, while the other boys cursed at me in a foreign language and spat on me. I can honestly say getting your butt whipped by a dancing teenager with a girly haircut sucks. Yet those boys were a minor disturbance, compared to the unrest the greater Los Angeles area experienced: the street-gang explosion and the hysteria over the AIDS epidemic that gripped the city with more fervor than the fear of what moved in the shadows when the sun went down.

Most nights during the first four months, as the moonlight poured through my window, I scoured the alley three floors below. I was convinced Richard Ramirez, the Night Stalker, was coming to get me. Two of his victims had lived and died in Glendale, their houses just a few blocks away. After my parents forced me to move to California, this seemed like a logical conclusion, death by serial killer.

The fear of a murderer on the loose in the Sunshine State was real to me. After all, my grandmother's cousin Butch killed more than a few people out here in the late '60s and early '70s. He stuffed their bodies into oil drums or something like that, young women and men who just simply disappeared until the cops caught Butch. The ballad of Butch was retold over pumpkin pie and holiday cheer. The way some members of the family tell the story, Butch either escaped or was released from prison and went back to what he knew.

During those early months, the Night Stalker was on everyone's lips: at the corner deli, the checkout line at Ralph's, bus stops, even the lunch line at school. I could not move ten feet without hearing his name. He kept me up at night, scared shitless. I slept with a steak knife. In the end, cops did not get him. One afternoon, normal citizens recognized him on the street. A footrace ensued and several men and women quickly encircled him and beat his ass to a standing ovation of onlookers. The cops came to the serial killer's rescue. Even though Ramirez deserved to be beaten, I felt bad for him. So many people cheered as the group punished him. I related to that feeling of being an outcast.

"If they're picking on you, maybe you should be more social," my mother suggested. "Show them who you are. You have a lot to offer, you're the life of the party."

The two crowning social achievements of my time in Cali: the night last spring when the Hoover School LAPD brought me home from a science class trip to Yosemite National Park. I brought weed and got a girl stoned who I had a crush on. Her friends freaked out and turned me in. The last month of the school year, I became the administration's poster boy for community outreach; recovering addicts came by to speak to me; the cop lunched with me several times; I fulfilled community service projects for the upcoming drug-awareness week programs. My favorite part was all the kids in my other classes talking about the incident. They described the bad person that turned Alison Wong onto drugs as if he was far removed from my reality. They called him some new person named *Jason*. One of the girls in my English class even asked me, "Hey, Tex, you know who that is?"

Just when I thought things could not get worse, Craig came to visit, a few weeks later, at the start of summer. My mom thought a familiar face might do me good. In a display of rebellion, we totaled my mom's car by driving across front lawns and crashing into a retaining wall. Craig and I drew an impressive crowd of cops wielding firearms, helicopters with spotlights, dogs, pissed-off homeowners, bystanders, and angry parents. I lived in California six months and no one other than the police paid enough attention to learn my real name. The number one irritation I carried around living in this state is that everyone, including my teachers, called me Tex.

"Well, were they making fun of you?" my mother asks again, as my stepdad exits the room.

"What do you think?" I respond.

"I think they were being supportive," she answers. "I mean the whole JV team stood up at once, they didn't give anyone else a standing ovation. It seemed very sincere." I can tell by the tone of her voice that she does not believe this. The same tone she used when she told me how happy I would be moving from Texas to Glendale, Glendale to Oak Park.

You are not that stupid and neither am I.

"They just recognize your achievement, lettering on the varsity as a sophomore is a big deal," she adds.

"Yeah, Mom, a big deal."

She is right, I did letter on the varsity team. Everyone who played lettered on the varsity. The point the JV team made was that I didn't earn the recognition. As a second-string receiver and cornerback, I only played on a few of the special teams. My stats were an impressive line of zeroes: zero catches for zero yards, zero tackles, and zero interceptions. My two brightest moments on the field were outstanding. First, in a game against Calabasas High, a mutant teenager held me on kickoff coverage, spinning me around a couple of times before hurling me into the ground. My head snapped back and I hurt my neck. I wore a brace for two weeks. Second, a few weeks later I ran onto the field during the pregame, as the cheerleaders held a paper banner supported by two PVC pipes on both sides. I was second through the sign, behind Bradley, the biggest boy on the team, and he hit the banner with such force the poles flew out of the cheerleaders' hands and right between my legs. In full stride, I did a complete somersault, in midair, landing right-side up without missing a step. I had no idea what was happening. The display of acrobatics was so impressive that the local cable television commentator remarked, "That was number twenty, Jason Carney, with a spectacular display of gymnastics." The JV team is right: I did not earn the recognition, but I did not ask for it either.

"The coach said nice things about you," she tells me. "He expects you to contribute a lot next season."

When my mom had called and registered me at Oak Park, she inquired about football. Hoover high's school cop suggested sports might be a positive outlet for my behavior. Ten minutes after speaking with the school secretary, the varsity coach called my mom back. He mentioned the talent within Texas high school football seventeen times in the three-minute conversation. After my mother explained to him my situation and the reason for our move, I earned my way onto the varsity team. The fact that he'd never seen me didn't matter because I was from Texas and sounded like a very pissed-off young man. I had not played football since the seventh grade. Then, I played three positions: end, tackle, and guard. I sat on the end of the bench, guarded the water bottles, and tackled anyone who came near them. I suck at football.

"I don't know what to tell you, Jason," she says, "I thought you did great."

Our house is only three hundred yards from the stadium; she only came to one game, the first one. My grandfather and uncle were visiting from Dallas, so everyone watched me stand on the sideline, while my team lost by thirty-five points. Not only did we play badly, we looked terrible: bright-yellow pants, brown jerseys with yellow numbers, and bright-yellow helmets with brown face-masks. Not that my skill level or uniform mattered. The team record was as horrible as we looked at 1–10.

I do not have any friends, and I have had several altercations with other boys during the year.

"You just need to try harder," she says, "interact with the other boys."

The most contact I have with anyone on the team is at the video store. One of the seniors—a good-looking blond surfer type, very popular, drives a hot car—works there. I go in three or four times a week and rent porn from the back room. We say hello, he does not check my identification, and we say goodbye. Interaction.

"If we put our minds to it, we can find a way for you to fit in out here."

I tired of my mother's lame attempts at concern. The simple solution: pick one place and stay there. Three different schools from the start of my first year to the beginning of my sophomore year is ridiculous. My mother is too complex for simple solutions, preferring drastic change to fix all ills, preferring indirect riddle conversations over asking the required maternal questions about how moving affects me and how it feels to be an outcast.

But the truth is, *I am tired of talking about everything; some things don't need to be examined, they just need to be personally addressed. Stay out of my business, I got this one.*

"We seemed to interact tonight, lots of positive interaction," I say, walking downstairs to my bedroom.

Tonight was humiliating, the most embarrassing moment of my life; everyone could see what was going on, the JV squad's intentions were more obvious than the fact I was the worst player on the team. Parents in the bleachers even said out loud, "Look, they are making fun of that boy." I swore to myself, as the coach handed me my letter and I stared into the thirty smart-ass grins of that standing ovation, absorbing every moment of their laughter and jeers: *They are going to eat this moment come the fall.* I resigned myself to the idea that this is my home; next season, they will stand up for me again.

They will not be calling me Tex. I have been practicing.

THE RED AND BLUE LIGHTS SWIRL through the silence of my car. In this four-square-mile area, you will find more cops than almost anywhere else in the city. There is never a normal traffic stop on these streets. Most of the officers are young; very few are of color. They hassle the dealers, mostly young black men, pulling them over and searching their cars with seemingly no cause or provocation. While they let the buyers, mainly white folks from the surrounding suburbs, come and go as if this neighborhood was one of Dallas' finest travel destinations.

My eyes shake in the rearview.

I should have stayed in the hotel.

The current of insomnia rolls across my face, an out-of-tune band clanks in my head. My hand fumbles to turn down the radio, which is already off. I am too tired to care about going to jail. I make a right turn into a parking lot. I forget to use my signal. Stuff the two large hundred-dollar slabs into the Burger King bag, under the burgers and napkins, on the passenger seat.

Had to get caught sometime. I'm glad C is not with me.

I grab a handful of fries from the bag, roll down my window.

The officer approaches me cautiously. I can hear each step clunk on the concrete. His utility belt jangles against his leg. He stands off to the back of my window. I make sure he sees me eating the fries. A flashlight illuminates the back of my head from the passenger side. His partner can see me, although I have no idea where he is. I turn around and greet the officer at my door with a smile.

"Everything all right, sir?" I say, chewing as I speak. As if I could be of service to these gentlemen.

"What you doing out here tonight?" he asks.

An obvious question, a white man driving through this neighborhood at two in the morning is only after one of two things—hookers or drugs. Or both. The situation seems obvious if the officer would only take time to look at me. Unshaven, oily skin, and eyeballs that bounce in my head as if they were on a swivel, everything about me screams crackhead.

I bet they saw me leave the apartments. They know the rocks are in my car.

"Looking for my cousin Viv," I say. "She works out here in the middle of the night."

I have this excuse ready every time I come to score at this hour, but I have not had to use my verbal skills in this neighborhood; I have been lucky. As many times a day as I roll through these streets, this should have happened a long time ago.

I will have to call Freeda, have her meet me at the jail instead of the hotel.

I do not think this excuse is going very far.

"She works out here?"

"She lives at the truck-stop motel across the bridge. Street walks to pay for her addiction," I say. "So I come out here two, three times a month to check on her—give her food, clothes, money, share a Christian word. Whatever she needs, just making sure she's still alive."

"Why so early?"

"Hard to find her in the sunlight; she's very nocturnal. Besides, I get up early. You might know her or seen her? Her name's Viv; she has one glass eye?"

"Glass eye, huh. You sure she is your cousin? You her customer?"

I am surprised. He acts as if he knows her. *Could I be this lucky?*

"Cousins, yes; customer, no. She used to babysit me," I say. "Have you seen her?"

"Babysit you, huh. She's a nice woman, struggling. Why do you want to get her in trouble by lying?"

"Her boyfriend shot her and left her for dead out in Forney. Five times, still has one bullet stuck behind her eye socket. Makes my grandmother feel better knowing I come out here and check in. Viv doesn't walk very well, has a hard time seeing. My aunt Bobbi is sick. Got to take care of family."

"All right, give me your license and registration. Sit tight, I'll be right back."

I feel anxious. *This was a stupid idea.*

The lights keep swerving around the cab of the car, a crowd gathers at the Racetrack gas station across the street. My car is recognizable in this neighborhood; all the panhandlers know my connection, know that I am C's customer. They keep close eyes on the interaction. Everyone here is constantly trying to get one up on each other; if they can score ten or twenty dollars' worth of crack by selling you out, they will. The vultures seeing me go down with two big rocks could be a bad thing. Crackheads—snitches around here. The sharing of information on the police and their activities, especially when it involves customers, can be profitable to a five-dollar hustler.

I reach into the bag for more fries; nonchalantly secure the sack so that a flashlight cannot see inside. A trip to the county jail not in my plans, I may have no choice.

There should not be any warrants for my arrest.

I can't remember any unpaid speeding tickets. I look in the rearview. The first officer joins the second at the front of the squad car. Their figures break the blue and red swirls as they talk. Their shadows bring me a sense of comfort inside my vehicle. I can hear them discussing, I cannot understand what they say. Each takes his side; the first one approaches my door.

"Do you have any drugs or weapons in the car?"

"No sir," I say, half laughing as if it's a ridiculous question. "Just a couple of Whoppers."

"Mr. Carney, we stopped you for failure to signal a turn," he states.

I know this is bullshit. I haven't turned in half a mile. I saw them pull out from a side street after I passed. The only signal I forgot to use was after they turned on their lights. The windows of my car are tinted. I suspect they thought a gangster was driving, late-night runner with a car full of dope.

"We are going to give you a warning tonight."

"Thank you, sir."

"I saw your cousin out here the other night," he says. "We cut her some slack, didn't have anything on her. She doesn't look too good. Said her mom is sick."

Viv, not right since the shooting, has a will to live that is something fierce. Sometimes I wonder if she wishes that she died that day. The amount of pain and struggle to relearn how to talk, hold a fork, her children's names. She amazes everyone by her victory. Her internal fortitude strengthened her so she could return to her heroin-cocaine addictions. Less than five years after her boyfriend shot her, she stabbed an old woman in the shoulder, in a Kmart dressing room for twenty-six dollars and a Social Security check.

Why did she fight so hard to survive?

"I worry about her, especially since her boys are back in jail," I say.

Viv has three boys, by two different men, all three younger than me, the oldest by just two years. My mom is stable compared to Viv; both were teenage mothers. I have not seen my cousins in a few years, mainly because they have spent most of their lives behind bars. Drugs, theft, and burglary, the calling cards of their criminal endeavors. Better inmates than thugs, they have never had the luck I seem to experience. I have spent most of my life thinking I am better than Mac, Jim, and Will. The truth is that our family has always occupied the bottom rung. We love them all, but some folks cannot be saved. Things were much simpler when we were kids.

"Well, I'll go by the hotel room," I say.

"Start to look in the daytime. It's dangerous out here. These people will kill you for five bucks. Drive safe, get home."

"I know. Some members of my family will sell their relatives out just to get high. Have a nice night, officer. Thank you again, sir."

WHEN THE TAVERN CALLS
1985

"DO YOU KNOW WHAT DAY IT IS?" HE ASKS.

The crackle of the phone line creates a deeper distance between us than already exists. Ten minutes ago, it was a normal Thursday. The phone rang at midnight so technically today is Friday, two in the morning in Illinois, where my father lives. I know he is referring to the day that just ended.

"Thursday," I answer.

"What kind of son are you?" he asks.

We have not spoken in almost three years. I did not know he could get ahold of us in California. When the phone rang a little while ago, I listened to my mom and stepdad Steve argue with him about being drunk. They did not want me to speak with him. He gets angry when drunk. I can hear the tavern linger over his lips.

"Well," he pauses, "don't even know today is your dad's birthday. What kind of son are you?"

That word makes me cringe. Dad. I long for him, defend him against my mother and the rest of my family, overlook the years of silence. The years that he wants to see me, birthday and Christmas packages arrive. Since my mom remarried, silence has been our primary bond. No different from the rest of my life. I know he loves me, I see our distance as my mom's fault. She has always been difficult.

"Happy birthday, I am so sorry, Dad," I cry. "I should

have remembered, I am so unhappy here, I miss you."

"Makes me feel like shit to know my own kid doesn't even know it's my birthday. I expect more from you, boy."

"I would never let them adopt me. I don't want Steve's last name. I like being Jason Carney. I am your son. I love you, Dad."

As I listened to them speaking after the phone rang, my mom told my father that Steve plans adopt me. They plan to change my last name. He would have no connection to me at all.

Fourteen, closer to a man than a boy, I stormed down the stairs, yelling that Roy is my father, blubbering like a wounded preschooler. I love him, they can never take that away. They gave me the phone and let me find out for myself. *I should have stayed upstairs.*

"Well, a good son calls his father, especially on his birthday. Not even a card. Your sister got me a card. A nice sweater too."

My half-sister is seven or eight; my stepmother bought those things. I hate his new family. Hate the fact that they have taken my place. Even when I am there with him, our time together is always my little half-sister, my father, and me. She gets him every day of every year. I get him two weeks every two years; even then, I do not truly get time with him. He never listens when I try to tell him what his absence means in my life.

"You didn't even call." His resentment builds.

I apologize repeatedly. Hysterical, I do not want to betray him; cannot forgive myself for not being a more loyal son. I crave his love and have chased his approval my whole life. I have seen the black eyes of my mother and stepmother. My heart knows he would never hurt me like that. My mind knows the damage is already done. I am still his little boy.

THIRD TIME IS THE CHARM
1987

MY DOWNFALL BEGINS in the first week of my senior year of high school back in Texas. By Thursday afternoon, I am a typical drug-addicted, disconnected teenager. Around nine that evening, my grandmother calls to tell me my mother is in the hospital again and that she and Steve are getting divorced. Neither piece of information surprises me. They fought three of the five years of their marriage. For the third time, my mother swallowed a bottle of pills, and that gave me permission to do whatever the fuck I wanted.

She gave no warning, which allows me a special visit tonight, since she was admitted straight from the emergency room. I pack a suitcase for her. In the main lobby my grandmother and I meet a doctor I have never seen. He escorts us down hallways and out into a courtyard, then over to her unit.

When we walk into her room she does not look into my eyes. Her breath is heavy, she is vacant. Barely able to sit up, her mascara covers her face and pillow. I smell the traces of vomit wiped on her sleeve. The doctor, not her normal shrink, tells us about multiple personality disorder and the erratic lives of those who succumb to this form of mental anguish. My mom fixates on the blanket wrinkled on her bed. I fixate on two facts as my mom gives me her credit cards and car keys, saying she will be home in a few months.

She is truly nuts. This doctor is the dumbest motherfucker in the world.

B AIT
1987

THE RAIN SLIDES DOWN MY CHEEKS and coats the parking lot a glossy shade of midnight, echoing the sky. The sheen of asphalt muddles the reflection of the neon signs. The edges of a gas puddle on the ground resemble a soft, muted watercolor. The sounds of early morning sweep down the highway. Large trucks crawl through the night like a rumbling mist. The parking lot smells crisp from engines cooling down as the rain evaporates off heated hoods. My breath escapes in small clouds, visible for a second before dissipating into the November night. I am nervous. I have never done this before. Tonight, I have to put in the work. Tonight, I am the bait.

"Remember, don't look anyone in the eye," Blue Eyes says. "Head straight to the back hallway, and walk slowly like you been here before. They won't say shit to you."

The goal is to get a man to drive away with me. They will follow in my car. When he stops, we will rob and beat the cocksucker. If I cannot get a man outside, I aim to go into a booth and overtake one there.

"It's dark as fuck inside. Don't get lost."

"I need a bump," I say. "Give me a bump."

"After, after," Blue Eyes replies. I've already had too many.

He punches me in the shoulder. He knows my stomach is up in my throat. Blue Eyes says, "Jason, they're going to love your cute little face. You're going to be real popular."

"You know I don't like it when the plan changes," I respond.

The plan, as we've done several times, was to go to the park and cruise for a man to pick up and rob. We call this game "Rolling Fags" while the police call it robbery and assault. It's very popular among boys from my side of Dallas. At least high school boys like us. The game is simple and requires only the slightest imagination and a little bait. The bait is the sucker who has to approach the men, the one who does all the talking and most of the fighting. I am normally the driver.

Our usual park being empty, we head to the porn store. With a movie gallery and coin-op booths in the back, men gather in the dark there, looking for a chance encounter. They enter the small booths with strangers to exchange sex. Older men, who relish the opportunity to teach a young man of my age the ins and outs of masculinity, saturate the darkness like a plague. Tonight I am the cure.

"Damn, they're crowded tonight, easy pickings." Blue Eyes looks over the parking lot, which is surprisingly full considering the weather. "Look at the watch before you choose. That's a good indicator of who has money."

We stand at the front of my car, the entrance twenty feet away. The coarse fibers of my sweatshirt stretch out like cottony hairs on the lips of a Venus flytrap. The light rain balls on the fabric; my sweatshirt is a flower covered in morning dew, awake and waiting for flies. I stand motionless, facing my terrible fear of dick-sucking faggots.

"If you get one in a booth, lock the door behind you. Wait for them to make the first move." He laughs. "Then spring the trap."

"Cool."

"Don't get on your knees," Blue Eyes smiles, "most importantly, don't suck a dick."

Mayor McCheese, Grimace, and the Hamburglar sit in the backseat. They take turns doing key bumps from a bag of speed. The windows start fogging. They stammer at the top of their lungs as if singing in round:

"Bring him outside."

"Get a fat one."

"Don't fuck up."

They cheer impatiently. Their yells muffled by the windshield, I barely understand them. My legs bounce. Adrenaline flows through me: nervous, cold, and unsure.

I hope I don't fuck this up.

"If nobody's in the rooms, pick one out of the hall. They won't be able to take their eyes off of you." Blue Eyes laughs again.

As he speaks, a cold and furious sensation climbs my spine. In the back of mind, I sense them touching me and my muscles clench. It feels dirty. Frozen breaths tingle at the base of my neck. I think I smell piss. I assume it is the parking lot.

"Dude, that is gross, I don't want them touching me," I flicker with anger, too scared to let it come forward.

"Tell them to take you somewhere quieter. We'll watch the door and follow in the car. Just be calm."

What if I don't remember any of this shit?

Blue Eyes is experienced. He is older, nineteen. He looks twenty-seven, a dropout with no idea what a job is or how to obtain one. He never has money but always has a plan. I do not know how I let them talk me into being the bait tonight.

"It's a rite of passage, a ritual of belonging," he says. "It's your turn, motherfucker! You better kick ass."

Doing this balances the fact they are crashing at my house, eating my food, and spending my money. The act makes me worthy to hang out with them. I do not care about these things; I just don't want to be alone.

My senior year of high school is a daily train wreck, in

slow motion. The downward spiral of the past few months has been surreal. I catch myself in awe, wondering how the fuck you make it stop. I have no fucking clue. My stepfather left, my mom tried to swallow a bottle of pills for the third time, and she's in the loony bin again. I live by myself. I rarely wake up and go to school. My father does not want me and when I think of him wanting me a feeling of sickness overtakes me. My house, the community center for all juvenile delinquent behavior happening in Mesquite, Texas, is where people come to do drugs, buy drugs, have sex, and crash. I am my own supervision. The reason I have so many fair-weather friends is that I am not very good at policing myself.

"Be quick about it; don't run when you leave. Stay calm. Don't forget the wallet." The speed took hold of Blue Eyes hours ago and he will not shut up. "Unless you're being chased."

"Hell yeah, I got this," I say. "They won't see it coming."

I have no idea what to expect.

CARNIVORES
1987

THE MOMENT I OPEN THE DOOR, perversity flows over me. The crisp humidity of outside falls away to the sticky current of electricity pulsing from the lights overhead. A film of water covers my body. I pause, look around the store, and take out a square.

Nothing says old enough to be in a porn store like smoking a cigarette.

My wet fingers fumble with the lighter. It takes the fourth strike of the wheel for the flame to erupt. I inhale deeply. The store is library quiet.

To my left is the counter. There is a man with brown hair wearing a green shirt. He studies me for a moment from behind the glaze of his glasses. He stands on the customers' side.

The way he looks at me, he is probably a cop or a security guard. He bends over and whispers something in the clerk's ear. *Great, they are going to kick me out.*

The clerk, a midtwenties slob, looks as if he has not taken a bath in days. He sits on a stool behind the counter reading a magazine. After a moment, the clerk looks up at me, smiles. His long curly black hair sticks out from under a greasy red and white ball cap that reads, *Motherfucker.* He then says something to the man and they both laugh. The guy in green slaps him on the shoulder and disappears behind a black curtain. I am sure they are going to kick me out.

An oscillating fan vibrates on the plate-glass counter; as it crosses his path, I smell a combination of boiled egg and hand lotion. A T-shirt two sizes too small does not cover the belly lying slack over his lap. The clerk hunches across the counter, rests an elbow on top of the display case. I expect him to ask for my identification. He does not, he returns to his magazine.

Looking down, he simply states, "No smoking." He points to the wall to my right and turns the page.

To my right is a large neon-green poster board. Handwritten on the sign, in thick black marker, are the words, *NO SMOKING*. A solid black arrow points down to an ashtray. Compliant, I bend over and jab my full smoke squarely into the ashtray. The chrome lid, not secured very well to the top, falls onto the floor. A crash reverberates throughout the store.

Motherfucker.

All eyes are on me. The clerk seems irritated.

"Sorry about that," I say.

The clerk rolls his eyes, and laughs as if to say, *Stupid kid.* I pick up the butts, place them in the bottom of the base, and secure the lid tightly. I then blow the fallen ash, spreading it across the floor. The clerk resumes his reading. I wipe my hands on my jeans, the store returns to quiet.

I fucked up. I was not supposed to be noticed.

Unsure of what to do, returning to the car a failure not an option.

My mind races at a meth-heightened pace. All my senses work overtime, my thoughts getting stifled under the beat of the light. The force of the current is so strong I swear I see the bulbs surge dark then bright. The whirls of the fan are a menacing cackle behind its sweet touch. Thin bursts of air invigorate my wet arms. My hair stands on end. Every sensation is euphoric.

To the right hangs a neon sign indicating an arcade. *Time to play some games.*

Music and groans waft out from behind the black curtain.

Between the curtain and where I stand, there are many aisles of pornographic movies. Each aisle houses hundreds, with hundreds more movies lining the walls on hanging racks.

I can do this.

At first, I do not register a pattern to the arrangements on the shelves. Then my eyes catch the box covers of naked chicks in various poses and sexual situations. That is all I need to know. I am more than curious to look at a few, and what seems to be a bright idea pops into my head.

Take a couple of minutes, look at the boxes, calm down, and work your way to the curtain slowly.

I begin to stroll through the aisles, without being too obvious.

I have to hurry. Just go to the curtain. Pick one of these guys. Oh, that chick is being wrecked. Look at that big-dick midget.

My thoughts move quickly and I forget why I am here. To the point of addiction, I have a penchant for porn. I have a favorite porn-star crush, Christy Canyon. She is tall and busty, one of the most beautiful women I have ever seen. So-phisticated and elegant, she never seems trashy or whorish in her movies, even when she takes two at a time. I look around for a box with her picture.

For a brief moment, the man in green sticks his head out of the curtain and makes eye contact with the clerk. The clerk motions to him with his hand, shaking his head. The only reason I notice is that they both stare at me briefly.

What is going on back there?

There are maybe six men browsing the aisles. I do not think they are suitable for my needs. Besides, none of them makes eye contact.

They must not be fags, I think. *Where the hell is every-one?* I know the answer already. *If I wait a few minutes, I bet the security guy comes back up front.* I continue browsing. *He is probably waiting for me to come back there.*

Excitement overtakes me as I find Christy Canyon on the cover of a bright red box. A movie I have never heard of before. She is just as I remember. A tall and naturally busty brown-haired woman with curvy hips and full lips. The look on her face exudes sex. She holds a giant stuffed animal between her legs. She straddles it like she killed the beast and it's a stuffed souvenir. She looks hot.

I would love to fuck those big tits. Stick my tongue down her throat and fuck the shit out of her. I turn the box over to see the hard-core snapshots displayed on the back.

"Oh shit!" I yell. "Goddamn! She's got a dick!" I throw the box on the floor.

That was definitely not Christy Canyon. Christy does not have a big hard dick.

Everyone in the store stares at me. The clerk stands up, stretches, and pulls his cap back to the rear of his head. He waits to see what I am going to do.

"Sorry about that," I say, and try to laugh it off.

I pick up the movie and return it to the shelf.

I am totally fucking this up.

I pick the movie up off the shelf again and study the weirdness of it all. I am perplexed, not believing that the girl pounding the dude on the back is the same soft woman on the front. I flip the box front to back, front to back, suspended in disbelief.

How in the hell is this possible? It is so fucking gross.

The eerie sensation from the parking lot returns.

I stand building disgust in my gut as I stare at the box. Control beams from her eyes as she peers into the camera. Her hands grasp his ass, giving him his reward. My mouth salivates with a warm liquid pool, the type that forms right before you vomit. My back hurts, the muscles surrounding my kidneys clench. There are mixed emotions stuck in the back of my throat.

I feel like I am going to hurl.

I imagine being the man with her hands on my ass. The emotion from deep within my body careens over and scares me. I feel a hidden bit of myself craving this punishment. I recognize part of myself in the picture. The Golden Ox Café and breakfast with my dad pops into my mind. I do not understand this random association. I flash to him sitting on the bed, tossing cards into a hat. Sporadic and specific, his actions are methodical and slow. My mind spins and I'm filled with anger.

Dude, you are freaking out.

Something is not right. I cannot stop my leg from twitching. My own thoughts disgust me. Disoriented, I hiss at the box and place it back on the shelf. I stare off into space frozen, fearful.

After a moment, the clerk resumes his reading, and the browsers browse. Now I am too frightened to make a charge for the curtain.

I am going to beat an ass-fucker tonight. Stop being a pussy. I can do this.

Since the clerk already knows I am in the building, I decide I will look at the contents above the counter, and then slide into the darkness. As I approach, I notice a selection of blow-up dolls, restraints, dildos, and fake vaginas shelved behind the clerk. The longer I am here the more fucked up this place becomes.

The imitation pussies look disgusting.

Made of molded plastics that resemble a round ass in the air, you mount the contraption from behind. Coarse fibers stick out the underside, beneath the enlarged hooded clitoris. The doll is designed after a real woman's body. You can have either the ass or the gash. Neither looks real. I cannot believe men actually pay for this thing, then take it home and fuck it.

What kind of sick fuck does that stupid shit?

Not paying attention to what I'm doing, I trip over the legs of the bargain bin in front of the counter. The large metal basket containing a few hundred movies shifts across the floor. A large ruckus ensues as videos fall from the overflowing bin. The clerk looks up at me and snarls. He starts to get up in a huff.

"I got it," I say, anxious and embarrassed.

Can you believe this bullshit?

My insides are knotted and confused, but I start to pick them back up, glancing at the covers. I take my time to make it seem that I was headed to the bin all along. Most of the films are compilations of fetish movies. Ugly women beat and fuck uglier men with dildos.

People are fucked up, I think, glancing at the curtain.

I can smell the black cloth and it reminds me of my father's apartment. There is an urgency now to unleash my fangs behind its cloak. A different form of saliva trickles in my mouth. Speed courses over my muscles like a twitch. My mind is hysterical. I look at another box, trying to keep it all together. This one is a video of lactating women who fuck on film to pay for their new babies. The edges of my sight blur with more disgust.

What kind of sick fuck makes a pregnant woman do that shit?

More giant cocks on big-breasted women, I skip that one. Super-hairy beavers and women with enormous nipples that are four inches erect. I try to laugh. The sound is manufactured and forced.

This is so fucked up.

Things are not going well. I was not expecting these distractions.

I have no idea how I am going to do this without causing

a scene. How I am going to explain my failure to my friends? What is going on with me?

For a moment, I try to figure my way out and not a path further in. I look at the clerk, puzzled.

He knows why I am here. He is going to call the cops. I have to be quick.

I consider asking him for a way out of this situation. Then I decide to ask if there are fags back there or not.

He probably gets sick of working around the cocksuckers all day. The thoughts running through my head are not very sound. *If he were going to bust me, he would have done it already.*

I decide to return to the car, figure that my clumsiness made a bust of the situation. Halfway to the door, I stop, turning back to face the arcade entrance.

"Hey," the clerk calls me over to the counter. "I am Wendell. Man, you ain't got to be so nervous if you want to go back there, man. Go on back." He pauses. "You can smoke in the booths, just make sure to put money in. No standing in booths that aren't running."

"Cool," I say, "anything else I should know?"

"There is a guy back there named Al. He's in a green shirt."

"The security guard?"

"No, man, he is just a customer, looking to make friends," he says. "He will show you where to go. Chill. You're safe here. No one is going to hurt you."

WHAT KIND OF FOOL PETS A VULTURE?
1987

I STAND WITH THE CURTAIN IN HAND. A delicate beam of light penetrates the greasy air. The cavernous room is pitch black. My eyes adjust. I make out the outlines of shadows; slowly, they become figures ambling down the hallways leading off the main space. Astonished, I see more than twenty men roaming through the blackness. Some notice the light and scurry into the shadows with one another. A few straggle. Those individuals stand by themselves minding their own business.

This large space is a maze of plywood, painted black and divided into booths. Each booth has a door and a number. The one closest to the curtain is number thirty-six. Groans and gravel-mouthed breaths intertwine with loud obnoxious porn soundtracks; every booth gives off its own collage of noise. The sheer lustful nature of the sounds is suffocating. My breath escalates and I feel the surge of my heart as I stand there.

It is darker than hell.

I do not like the dark, never have. The idea of the lights going off, as the degenerates slither toward me with forked tongues, brings a burning sweat to my palms.

I can do this. Don't flip out.

Completely overwhelmed, I look for a direction. There are two. I can travel right, down a short hall that seems to turn left; or straight ahead, down a longer one trailing off into more darkness. Options noted, I inhale deeply, focus my vision on the darkest part of the room, and assure myself bad things are not happening to me. I release the curtain.

I hear a man laugh. Four guys stand off to my left, under the lone black light that marks the exit. The man in the green shirt is one of them. He laughs again. He sees me and nudges a tall, bizarre, wiry man. His white T-shirt and bleached-blond curly hair glow in the heat of the black light. The strange luminescence, highlighted by his heavy tan and light-blue eyes, makes him appear inhuman; his arms seem longer than his legs. He looks like an albino ostrich from outer space. They both watch me with smiles. Their lips, emitting sinister whispers, glow in the dark like bird feathers against the sun. The oils glisten across the hollow fibers in shimmers of pink-yellow-blue. They cackle hungrily. I cannot hear what they are saying, but it is about me.

Fucking faggot pedophiles.

My skin crawls as they scour me with their eyes. The fact that they congregate in groups leads me away from them.

Maybe in the parking lot with Blue Eyes and the other three guys in the car, but alone, I just need one.

I walk slowly down the corridor to my right. The back of my head tingles. I know they are still watching me.

Gross-ass fucking faggots. I bet those assholes have a circle jerk.

The first few booths I pass are empty.

I glance into the open doors. Each one identical: a television monitor, multiple movie channels to choose from, a folding metal chair, a small chain attaching the chair to the wall; a chrome generic paper towel dispenser, hung on the wall at eye level; and an ashtray, exactly like the one at the front door. Most of the tight spaces smell like piss and mildew. Butts litter the floors, some glued to drops of gooeyness.

It is just too fucking weird.

A booth tucked into the corner on the right catches my attention. It is three-quarters open with a man standing on the folding chair. I stop. He looks through a peephole to the adjoining unit. His pants are down. He is going to town. Stunned by the fact that he fondles himself as he watches, I clench my jaw, mesmerized.

There is something about his hands.

To me, his long and sharpened digits resemble talons. Out of the corner of his eye, he sees me spying on him. I do not move. He turns his bearded face to me, unblinking, owl-eyed terror in his gaze. He looks possessed. Without letting go of his penis, he lifts his right leg off the chair. Perfectly balanced, he kicks the plywood door. The black wood slams shut. I move on.

Three doors down the hall, the darkness actually takes shape. The air is colder. I become disoriented, my sense of direction skews, and I do not feel safe. The darkness above me is suddenly loud and alive—as if a million pellet guns are firing at the same target.

It must be pouring outside.

All of the doors on this side are closed. No one lurks. But then I hear something behind me and I turn around. Down at the end of the corridor, the man in the glowing white shirt leans against the booths to the left, smiling.

Getting pretty creepy.

I will choose him.

I stand at a left turn. Suddenly, I understand the maze. The arcade is set up in a big square, four hallways that connect. Lining both sides of every corridor are the pay-per-view booths. There are three doors on the right side and two on the left in this section of the square. The middle booth on the right has a man peeking at knee level into a hole in the door. He taps on the surface, as if he has a secret knock. I stop.

The door opens. The light from the monitor illuminates the hallway. I see a hairy man sitting in the chair, shirtless. Sweat and clumps of coarse hair cover his torso. Pants down, his large erection in plain view. The squatting man scoots into the room. Before the door closes, I see his mouth open around the head, cock already in his hands.

I am going to throw up. This place is like being on another planet. *I have to get out of here.*

"Looks good, don't it?" The man in white stands a couple of feet behind me. "What's your name?" He moves toward me.

I move forward without speaking.

Get the fuck away from me, you freak. My stomach flips with what I just witnessed. I turn left again.

This hall leads to the spot where I came in thirty feet away, brighter than the rest. I can see clearly the other three men standing at the black light. The curtain sways as some men exit. Between us are three other men standing in the hallway. I feel like everyone is eyeing me. I stop and peer over my shoulder. The man in white stands smiling, his teeth seem to float in the dark. I feel trapped.

I have to get away from this dude.

I pick an empty booth halfway up, across from one of the three men; I enter and lock the door.

The longest walk of my life.

Out of breath, facing the door, my mind frazzles, unable to comprehend what went wrong.

Blue Eyes was right, I am fucking popular.

They stalk me like vultures, circling for the kill. I am a dying carcass for their delight. There is a tap on the door. The slide lock screwed into the plywood rattles with each sound. I imagine a beak's soft pecks, looking for entrails. I imagine a line forming out in the hall. They pass the secret knock to one another so they all will get a turn.

I cannot stay here.

The tapping stops.

"PPPSSSTTT!" comes a voice from the other side. Fingers once again snap the door; the vultures' pursuit escalates.

"Hey, let me in!" I recognize the man in white's voice.

This shit is getting out of control.

"Go away!" I say loudly.

There is silence. My mind contorts with fear. I try to remember Blue Eyes's instructions. All I can think of is that he should have given me another bump. I hear another voice from the hall.

"Chill out, Stan, you're scaring him. Don't be so pushy."

"Whatever," White T-shirt says. "Shouldn't come back here if he doesn't know what he wants."

"Leave the kid alone. You're going to ruin it."

"Don't worry, boy, if you got a small cock. You're here to suck them," he laughs.

"Damn, that is cold," another voice interjects. "I'm out of here."

"All of them." There is a slur to his speech. I can tell he has been drinking. He does not seem so menacing now. I know that weak men bow up reckless with violence under the protection of liquor. The rain fires down harder.

There are a few giggles. I hear footsteps heading down the hall. Inside, I laugh nervously at my predicament.

What kind of man are you? They are the ones here to suck dick, you're stronger than those drunken fuckers.

I am terrified Blue Eyes will come in here and find me hiding in a booth. I will never live it down if they have to come save me. A moment of truth's spike of courage takes hold of me. I steady myself for the fight outside the door.

I am not backing down from these cocksuckers.

I open the door. Our foreheads connect.

The green and white shirts look surprised. A shorter, more

subservient-looking fellow with very little hair and big ears seems uninterested in the whole situation. He gazes in the direction of the black light. I hear two voices at the exit. The clerk and another fellow raise the curtain. A shard of light stabs the darkness. For a moment, I see everyone's face.

Fucking scavengers.

They don't scare me anymore. The man in the white T-shirt chuckles.

"Boo!" a voice utters through a twisted snicker. A man slides out of the open door next to my booth. He tries to startle me. We make eye contact. He laughs under his breath; beads of liquid stain his forehead. I see him clearly; he looks more creepy than harmful. There are four men, but only two concern me.

I will not run.

I smile.

"Fuck y'all," I say under my breath.

I cannot let these faggots have power over me.

I back up into the booth, waiting to see which one will join me. My heart pounds in the bottom of my throat, no turning back. The shadow of the room envelops me. I don't have to wait long.

The man in the green shirt steps through the doorway. Surprised that it is not the man in white, I feel a little disappointed. Barely enough room for us both, I slide up against the wall. My knees lock. I reach out and close the door. Secure the flimsy bolt. Position my body on the door and the wall. I panic. I stop breathing. My lungs seem full of water, I am scared to move for fear that it will be a sign of acquiescence. He smiles at me. I stare into the sound of the rain above me.

Everything moves at half speed. I feel light-headed, my breathing rate increasing. We stand there, in a mostly dark closet, separated by twenty inches of space. I do not want to look at him. The silence is so consuming, a nauseating gurgle of warm bile pools in the back of my throat. He pulls out some cash and inserts it into the coin-op slot.

The monitor comes to life, the booth is illuminated.

"That's better," he says. His focus is on the control panel as he searches for a film to his liking.

The images move so quickly it is hard to tell what is what. A breast, a mouth, some hair, a pair of eyes, a close-up of penetration, a couple talking, more penetration, an orgy, some credits rolling on a black screen, eyebrows, a man's head buried in a woman's lap, a car, two girls fucking, a man's ass, a hand holding a vibrator—his thumb comes off the button. The screen halts.

A man in a police uniform stands outside a jail cell while a young male prisoner, on his knees, sucks him off through the bars. I cannot take my eyes off the vulgar display.

"Yeah, that looks good," says the man with glasses and the green shirt. He peeps at me, tongue between his crooked teeth and thin lips. "What do you think?"

I do not respond. My eyes twitch from the monitor to his face. I don't know where to look. Slurps and wheezes radiate out from the speakers at full volume; I close my eyes, the echoes paint a picture that I cannot get out of my head. When I open my eyes, the man in green rubs the outside of his jeans; squeezes down tighter on the tip of his tongue. I stand completely frozen.

"Well then," he says. The channel changes, I can hear a woman's voice.

On the screen, a women's long brown hair bounds over a man's lap.

What am I waiting for?

Bewildered more than angry, I watch the film and ignore my companion. Something about the girl's face seems familiar. He changes his stance, feet farther apart. He coughs. An

anxious grin covers his face, his hands now inside his unzipped pants.

You have to do this.

He looks down at his crotch, then at me as if to suggest I
should get to work. I glance down at mine, then right in his
eyes. I whisper, "Show me how?"

He smiles and salivates. I ball up my hand in anticipation.
My knees twitch, my whole body shakes—a tired swimmer
with hypothermia, flailing, lost in rough waters. The enormity of the situation swells, I do not know if I am in control.
My knees still locked, every muscle tense; I cannot move my
body. We stand face-to-face. I am in the water torture tank
from which Houdini escaped, upside down and out of oxygen. This booth the size of a shoe box.

I can smell his breath as he passes my face on the way
down. Stale smoke and coffee, the filmy stench is like a fester-
ing sore. Suddenly his breath reminds me of my father and a
terrified anger consumes me. He puts his hand on my chest.
I think of pancakes and thick slices of ham covered in syrup.
His touch takes all the breath out of me. I feel like a little
boy. My back seizes with pain, I sense fangs crawling over
my skin. I am trapped and cannot move, pressed up against
the wall. He slides his hands down my abdomen, the button
pops open; my mind snaps to the most vivid burn, I feel like
I am on fire.

Something takes hold of my body and I am watching
myself from overhead. My sense of time distorts. I cannot
breathe. I can feel him hovering in front of my midsection. A
cold sensation runs over my penis. I gasp. I grow inside his
mouth. I am numb.

The only thing keeping me from drowning is the video
screen. The warm sensation of his mouth is macabre. I am
lost in the girl on the screen. She looks so hot and incredibly
beautiful; my mind searches for any plausible connection to

what is happening. The girl in the video stands and for the first time I see her ass, perfect and round, the shape of a heart. I am fully erect. She opens her legs and a large cock falls out. I realize she is the woman on the red box. I flinch and look down. My father's eyes, mouth full, staring up at me.

"NO!" I scream at the top of my lungs, awake to what is happening.

In one furious movement, I grab his hair and pull his face back. I jam my left hand down and hear the cracking sound of his glasses. He crumples backward. Seven or eight more blows land on his face. A few bounce off the black walls. My knuckles splinter. My knee pins his head to the wall, it sounds like a balloon popping. The sensations I feel remind me of the little girl I babysat years ago, her flotation ring destroyed, her blue eyes bulging in unison with the twitches of her legs. In the midst of the frenzy everything is still and serene, my mind processing events it has not thought of in years. This is a baptism. I hover above him, my talons exposed. His eyes are squeezed shut; his arms are up, trying to shield himself. My punches turn to kicks.

"Fuck you, faggot!" I yell, lost in rage. "You want to suck my dick now?"

"Stop! Please!"

"Pedophile. Molester."

He whimpers. My hands brace the wall in front of me for traction. I kick him without mercy. The booth shakes and vibrates like a diving board recoiling from a diver's release; the plywood wall cracks. The ruckus of the exploding box fills the arcade.

"Dick-sucking faggot! Pedophile asshole!" I yell as I pick up the chair.

Tan and metal, the same kind of folding chair as in my church dining hall. Both chairs take part in acts of salvation. Blood on his face, he tries to scoot under the monitor, nowhere to go. I jab the base of the chair into his body. He wheezes with the impact. He endures this affliction, each new thrust less potent than the last. My muscles are exhausted at the release of my past. I am near the point of tears, the kind that come from happiness, or a healing moment. A weight lifts from around my body. I feel whole.

"Want to suck my dick now?" I ask again, out of breath, a cold sweat covering me. A boisterous smile spreads across my face. "This is what happens when you fuck little boys."

He doesn't speak. Spittle flies out of my mouth, landing on my chest and arm. I feel so alive. I unlock the door. There is no one in the hallway.

THIS DAY IS NOT STARTING OUT WELL. Barely able to stay awake, I lurch over the steering wheel. My right hand covers my right eye. The blinding haze is unbearable. I am only able to lift my head and focus my one good eye for a second or two, every twenty feet or so. I drive at half the speed of the traffic around me. The circular wound where the hot pipe jabbed into the corner of my eye a few hours ago throbs as if it were Mount St. Helens saying hello to the world. To those around me I must seem like an old woman moving through a school zone. The sound of the hazard lights clinking on and off in a metallic, robotic pulse annoys me.

My hand does not stop the liquid from oozing down my face. The glare of the sun wreaks havoc on my eye as the flesh around it swells shut. I need to find a hole to crawl inside of and escape the warm cheery thorns of morning. A thick curdle of tears rolls down my unshaven cheek. I am a vampire, melting. My car swerves under the pressure; the honks of the motorist behind me are as irritating as the bumps on my raw tongue.

I smell like shit.

C's place is ten minutes away. If I continue at this pace, I will arrive around noon. Out of dope, patience, and the ability to withstand the pain, I decide to pull over and get some Visine. A gas station looms on the other side of the intersection, two lanes to the right. When the light changes from green to yellow, I floor the gas. Somewhere in the back of mind, I have a hunch this is the best action. The car flies through the inter-section, across the two lanes, barely missing another vehicle running the light, and slaps the pothole at the corner of the entrance. My body jars with the impact. Sweaty, congested, and nauseated, my world spins with a singular purpose.

Get your shit together; go get your dope.

I pull into the shade of the building. The hairs on my arm stand upright with a twinge. I grab the handle as a woman walks out of the door, coffee in hand. Her polyester suit re-minds me of my grandmother.

Freeda is probably at the front desk by now.

I am shameless in abandoning my grandmother. While she travels halfway across Dallas this morning to rescue me, I travel two miles from where she lives to hide. The woman with the coffee smells of sickly sweet flowers and powder. I taste the alcohol of her perfume as I walk through the door and approach the counter. My grandmother disappears from my thoughts. My one eye scans the store, spots the aisle of aspirin and hygiene products.

"There it is!" I say loudly. "In business."

I fumble with cellophane-covered Visine package, crushing the box more than freeing the contents. My fingers are useless.

"Come on, fucker! Open the fuck up!"

The whole store is now aware of my presence, even the construction crew over at the coffee pots shake their heads at my nonsense. I gnaw at the edges of the package with my teeth. Saliva builds, coats the glossy rectangle as if it were a bone in the jowls of a large unkempt dog.

"Goddamnit!"

"Excuse me, sir," the clerk starts.

I stare him down. Before uttering his next sentence, his facial expression shifts. "Damn, your eye is really fucked up!"

I ignore him. The plastic tears, my hands are wet with spit. I wipe the grime on my jeans.

Now my hands are sterile.

Plastic wrap clings to my palm as I lift the bottle above my eye.

"You need to pay for that, sir."

"In a minute. Emergency," I respond.

The liquid fills the irritated mess. The stream pushes the thick film out, my eye floods with relief, the cool sensation a temporary fix.

"That's it," I say. "Hell yeah, that feels good!" In the middle of the store, helping myself, the bottle half empty when I lower it.

Just get me to where I am going.

"Woo, that feels good," I tell the clerk. "How you doing today? Busy morning, everyone headed to work."

"Man, your eye is gross," he responds. "You burn it? What happened to you?"

"A death in the family. Four packs of Marlboro Lights, please."

He heads to the sink behind the counter, grabs a handful of paper towels, runs them under the water. I notice a rack of sunglasses and grab a pair. A quick glance, the glasses are a man's style, all set.

"Here, that Visine isn't going to help you." He hands me the dripping paper towels.

"You care if I hang in the parking lot until I can drive?"

"Once you pay you can do whatever you want," he says. "You need to go to the doctor. You look like a leper."

I hand him the money, nodding, I have no time or patience to deal with his sarcasm.

"I need to go to sleep," I say, laughing as I step to the door.

In the car, the laughter fades. My situation is bleaker than I allow myself to realize. I pushed my body as far as I could. Still, I plan to go farther.

I fold a paper towel into a large wet square and force the light-brown, industrial-strength mess up against my eye. The cool sensation relaxes me. My shoulders release, the tension of the past few nights crawls over my bones. I shake. For a brief moment, I feel like my insides are glowing. As I tear the tag from the sunglasses, I notice tacky flames running down the sides. I do not care what they look like as long as they block out the sun. I have not smoked in almost an hour. My stomach grumbles.

Food and sleep.

My cell phone rings. C sends me a text, annoyed that I need to come over so early. I fumble through my money.

Two hundred—I better hurry.

The pain becomes bearable under the heightening of my urge. I throw the car into drive, my one good eye focuses, and my body cranes forward.

NOTE TO SELF:
TWENTY-SIX DAYS HIGH IN A HOTEL ROOM

Junkies' wisdom is a fractured wish,
a distorted angel-absent language,
a premonition that reiterates
squandered yesterdays.
Unholy, burnt-tongue psalm.

Junkies' wisdom is a boisterous lesion.
It exudes limitless ideas of resurrection,
walks with purpose of death
on crack-tear palms.

Junkies' wisdom is an irrepressible,
sinister devotion. A voluptuous
one-eyed stare into oblivion.
A butterfly

pulling apart his fucking wings.

T HE PRIZE
1979

I WANT A PARTY LIKE THIS ONE, SOMEDAY.

I feel proud in my light-brown suit, blue shirt, and thick polyester brown-and-blue-striped tie. My hair feathers to perfection, my shoes are without a scuff. The church fellowship hall buzzes under decorations. Streamers and balloons hang from the plywood walls in a carnival of colors without scheme. Thin plastic tablecloths wrap the folding tables, topped by purple and white arrangements of silk flowers. Toward the far side of the room, near the kitchen entrance, the tables of potluck scent the room. An excitement bubbles within me. My whole family crams into this small party room. Church members, Papaw's colleagues, and a few close neighbors.

Tonight is a very big deal.

Mamaw and Papaw stand against the far wall. Papaw wears his Sunday suit, the black one. Mamaw wears a light-blue polyester dress with a soft silk shawl the same color wrapped around her shoulders. This little old woman with more girth than height looks uncomfortable receiving so much attention. She is the center for almost every person in the room. I have never known anyone as loved by his or her family. He towers over her, hands bigger than her head. They look wonderful together. Old and full of life, their pride reflects back to them from the faces in the room.

A line of guests to their right pass and shake hands, each group taking a moment to pose for a quick picture in front of their cake. I observe the respect in all of the guests' gestures as they congratulate them on their success. Papaw and Mamaw never show affection to one another in public. I catch him glancing at her like a schoolchild with a crush.

"You look beautiful, Mamaw," he says. "The Lord sure has blessed us."

She blushes, extends her arm to the next in line, ignoring his compliments. They are simple people with simple dreams. Faith and family govern their world.

"Jason, come get in a picture," Papaw says, noticing me watching them.

The line stops as I make my way over to them. Three fast steps into a slide across the linoleum on the slick bottoms of my new shoes. My arms open, fingers pointing to the air as if I am shooting guns. Proud that all eyes are on me, that Papaw chose me to be in a picture.

"This is my oldest great-grandchild," he tells the guests I don't know. "Debbie's son."

I feel the love he holds for my mother as he rubs my shoulders with his large worker's hands. Mamaw reaches down and holds a napkin out to my mouth.

"You got a little crust on your lips," she says. "Spit."

I lightly spit into the wad of tissue and she scrubs the corners of my mouth.

This is so embarrassing.

"Jason, you look sharp tonight," Papaw swells. "Strapping young man. Going to be a prizefighter someday."

I don't know what he means. I don't care. He tells me this all the time. I trust he knows what he is talking about. I tell myself that what he speaks is true. I stand full of pride between them. They are the only people in the world that would never hurt me, never speak a cruel word to me.

"Just like me, son," he continues. "I found the prize worth fighting for, fifty years ago. Luckiest prizefighter in the world."

The flash pops, my eyes blink in a brilliant haze. The outlines of the people in the room radiate beyond the boundaries of their flesh. For a brief moment, everything around me is made of light. The instant is euphoric, as if we are close to heaven. Both of their arms cradle my neck. I feel like they will always be with me right at the back of my being. I know God is a line of blood relatives—they stand single file behind me. Their spirits connect to my soul; they breathe life into my dreams. They give their breath for me to live. I can hear the awe of my mom, grandma, aunts, and cousins. This photograph is precious. They both squeeze me in a formidable hug. I think I know what the prize is now.

I want to have a party like this one day.

IN THE DARK
1988

LAKE RAY HUBBARD LIFTS HIS FACE MID-SNORT, the straw hangs out of his nose so that he looks like a one-tusked walrus. His dilated eyes have a perplexed look as a few granules plummet out of the end of the tube and back onto the glass-topped table. My gaze fixates on the ceiling and the heavy footsteps erupting from my grandparents' bedroom on the second floor, a thousand miles away from what is happening in their living room and kitchen, but only a thirty-second walk. I am frozen. My heart races.

This could be bad. Really, really bad.

"Someone's coming," I say.

"No shit," he replies.

We both instantly look at the kitchen table, which is covered in powder cocaine, a scale, a scoop, and some baggies. We think it looks like Al Pacino's desk in the movie *Scarface*, though it's only two eight-balls. This is a normal Sunday night. We bag and weigh all the twenties out for the week, set aside what is ours to snort, and get any ready we intend to trade to the neighbor for weed and speed. My grandparents go to bed at ten, so around midnight we usually proceed uninterrupted.

"I hope it's Freeda," Lake Ray says.

We both do. I can always sweet-talk my grandmother. My grandfather scares the shit out of me. His silence is very threatening.

"Put up the weed," Lake Ray Hubbard says. "I got this. Put these in your pocket."

I move into the living room with the Tylenol bottle full of little white amphetamines that he just handed me. The bag of weed is on an old *Happy Days* television tray I ate dinner on as a kid. I shove the tray under the couch and the bottle of pills between the arm and the cushion. I glance over at Lake Ray. He carefully arranges two plates upside down over our inventory and drapes a thin cotton tablecloth, previously shoved out of the way, over our mess. Then he turns off the kitchen light. The blue glow of the television engulfs the room. Lake Ray smiles confidently at me as he takes a seat in the recliner at the edge of the room. He leans back and the squeak of the rusty springs echoes the footsteps approaching the bottom of the stairwell.

"Jase, you alone?" my grandmother asks from the darkness of the other room.

"Lake Ray is here," I say in a whisper, trying to appear considerate and quiet.

"Oh, okay." She's standing at the entrance of the living room. "What you boys doing?"

"Hey, Freeda," Lake Ray whispers. "Watching Pink Floyd's *The Wall* on MTV."

Out of the corner of my eye, at the far end of the couch, I see my grandmother clenching her purple robe shut in her left hand. I turn to look at her and smile.

She is not wearing her glasses.

I love my grandmother very much, but she does not see well, even when she is wearing her glasses. She wears spectacles for reading, but sometimes truly seeing requires too much effort.

"Are we making too much noise?" I ask. "We'll turn it down. You can go back to bed. We'll be quiet."

I have been loud since I moved in here a couple of months

ago. The downward spiral of my senior year covered three addresses. Here so that I could receive supervision, since my attempts at living on my own at the previous two houses were failures. After my mom got out of the loony bin, she gave our house back to my ex-stepdad as part of their divorce settlement. My mom and I moved into a small two-bedroom garden house. She left for Florida and a new job shortly after. My ex-stepdad got the first house that was ever ours. My mom got "healthy" and a chance to start over. I got the shaft, a two-bedroom garden home and a credit card to buy food.

She actually said to me, "I don't think it would be right for you to move halfway through your senior year." After twenty-three different addresses, and fourteen school changes in twelve years, this was my mother's way of saying, *I am living my life and you are not invited.*

To celebrate, I threw the biggest party Mesquite had ever seen. Lake Ray Hubbard and I charged a three-dollar cover at the door for a keg and two thirty-two-gallon drums of trash-can punch. Earlier in the day we made a smart decision by moving all the furniture into one room. We collected almost seven hundred dollars. The small neighborhood convulsed with mayhem. Kids were everywhere. End-to-end cars blocked everyone's driveway. You do not have to be popular to throw a good party, just offer teenagers the chance to get drunk and fuck shit up.

The police came the first time at about ten thirty. They emptied the place. I acted innocent, as if hordes of uninvited teenagers had taken over the house. Never mind that they all carried fliers with a map I'd printed at Kinko's. Some other kids started reproducing them for me at their schools. Thirty minutes after the cops left, the party doubled. Kids brought their own booze. Everyone drank, smoked pot, or got with someone upstairs. The shit was out of hand.

What do I care, not my fucking house. We are getting healthy.

When the same cops came back a second time after midnight, they found my grandmother and aunt beating kids into the street with their purses. Grandma came looking for my fourteen-year-old cousin, who was drunk with some girls upstairs. By that time, I was at the Waffle House tweaking my balls off.

The party was infamous: so much so that Lee Ann Henry, cheerleader and outstanding Christian, called me on the phone the following Tuesday night to pray with me. I was surprised she knew my name. I took the phone call as a sign of success more than an opportunity to overcome failure.

A week later, my mother gave me a stern warning over the telephone. I made sure to thank her for finally being happy and healthy. I was poison and getting away from me paid her big dividends.

Now I am living back at my grandma's for the first time since third grade. My grandparents can't deal with me. I should not be their responsibility anyway.

"No, y'all are fine. I just need a glass of water," she says. "What is this crap you're watching?"

My grandmother seems perplexed and enthralled by the cartoon cult classic. Without taking her eyes off the screen, she moves around the sofa and sits on the edge.

"This is weird, hammers marching." She squints deeper into the screen.

I squint deeper over Lake Ray's shoulder, into the darkness of the kitchen.

Go back to bed.

I trace my tongue along the upper ridge of my gum line, the cocaine creating a numb sensation all over my mouth and nose. At the back of my throat, I taste the gasoline snot stuck to the walls. Lake Ray and I keep making eye contact and cannot sit still. We fidget and giggle like two junior high kids.

Between the movie and the cocaine in my veins, I am having a hard time keeping it together. My grandmother seems unfazed and unaware. She sits in silence studying the images.

"This garbage will rot your mind."

"Pink Floyd, Grandma. This movie is a classic."

"More like hippie drug stuff. I am too old for this shit, giving me a headache. I need an aspirin and some sleep," she says, rubbing her forehead.

Almost as if by intuition, she reaches behind her and grabs the bottle of pills stuck in the cushion. I am in awe. Lake Ray kicks me in the leg and motions at her with his eyes in a panic. My grandmother caresses the cap to the bottle like a toddler. The darkness makes it hard for her to open it. She pauses.

"You burn something?" she asks.

"We were smoking out the back door," Lake Ray responds. "Those are mine, Mrs. Arnold. Dude, open that bottle for your grandma."

"Let me get that for you." I leap to my feet.

"I got it," she says, moving the bottle out of my reach. "It smells funny in here, too much smoke. Jason, your grandfather wouldn't like you smoking in the house. Don't make me get on you boys."

She smiles, stands, and walks over to the back door. She looks out the window of the door, unlocks then opens it. Again, she fumbles with the bottle cap.

"Let me help," I say.

"I can do it. I am blind, not old!" my grandmother snaps. "Jason, you need to lower the glass on the screen, get some fresh air in here."

"Sorry, Mrs. Arnold," Lake Ray says.

She walks into the kitchen, grabs a glass from the cabinet; the door slams shut a little hard for this time of night. We hear my grandfather restless in his bed above our heads, then silence. The water runs out of the sink slowly. My mind is racing.

That shit will kill my grandma. She is going to trip her balls off. I have to piss. Tell her the truth.

She is silent in the shadows, as if this is an act she has done countless times in the past. I move to the edge of the kitchen praying for the best possible outcome.

"Damn thing is pissing me off," she says, turning toward me, glass of water in hand. "If I didn't have a headache before, I got one now."

She moves over to me, kisses me on the cheek, and heads into the fishbowl glow of the living room.

"Forget it, too much effort," she says to Lake Ray as she passes him on her way to the stairs. She tosses the bottle into his lap. "I got some upstairs. Thank you anyway. You boys got school in the morning. Don't stay up late."

"Will do, Grandma."

"Yes, Mrs. Arnold."

"I am going back to bed. Lake, don't let him do anything stupid. Y'all keep watching stuff like that and people will think you're doing drugs or something."

BRUISED

We are reflections,
retreating from ourselves
into one another. Anointed
in a prophecy—
gratification.

A communion—
            flesh bought with a dowry
of symbols. Our eyes widen, burst with sleep.
We tread water. Rip the surface of the sun. A bone
sulfur flame emerges from our bellies
as we come in out of the cold.

We are born of language.

Laughter a sound we never utter. We stand
at the edge of dreams, deciphering the signs
that are left for us. The world is a glimpse.

Men are the scar of time's mistake.
Sleepwalking through the fog,
covered in pearls and urine stains.

CLANK
1988

"FUCKING WITCHES! FUCK YOU!" Yardstick yells.

"Witches!" I scream.

"Gonna get you tonight!" Cuban adds.

The car headlights cast shadows from our teenage arms extended into crosses onto the brown jungle of a front yard of the lavender two-story house. A four-foot wall of weeds guards the entrance, where there is no grass, no fertile foundation for this dwelling to be called a home. Only a forest of stickers and twigs, soda cans and discarded chip bags, overgrown shrubs and the vines of knotted plants baked in the summer sun until they crusted on the ground. The house sits right between two manicured and pristine homes on a quiet street with a big curve in a slowly impoverishing suburb. The best years are behind this town and monstrous structures like this prove it. The exterior gives the appearance of vacancy, but in the back are two late-model cars, both hunter green, one a Mercedes the other a Bug. We are convinced witches live here.

"Fuck you, bitches! Going to shoot you, witches!" Yardstick repeats, smiling at his drunken-ecstasy rhyme.

He stands on the sidewalk, focused on the front door. Eighteen and muscular, he is reckless and not afraid of anything. When he amplifies this courage with booze and drugs he is damn near unstoppable. He is the kind of man who is not long for this world. I dream of being that brazen. Tonight, he set his mind on having a good time with the crossbow he made in woodshop. The weapon balances in his right hand as an extension of our off-kilter imaginations. We are fucked up a lot.

"Come out and play, witches!" I yell as I throw my half-full beer can toward a window.

I rush up a small incline through the brush to the place where I think it landed. The dehydrated lawn snaps like potato chips under my shoes. The sound is as irritating as the itchiness of the weeds against my sweaty legs. Once I find the beer can, I take more precise aim.

The can thumps against the lavender siding; a large circle of wetness smears across the panels. I throw my arms into the air as if I just won the Super Bowl. I run back down to the street in exaggerated giant steps. I move like an awkward, overgrown child.

"Whores, scumbags!" the Cuban yells. "I am so fucked up!"

We are cartoonish tonight. I look over at the Cuban, the oldest of the group, his face covered in sweat. His pupils are two black holes swimming in the darkness. The white T-shirt he wears is matted to his torso while his right arm rubs his chest as if it's the softest thing he ever touched. His jaw is clenched as his head rolls side to side.

"Cuban!" I yell, stomping in his direction.

"Fuck you, witches, I feel good!"

"Throw something," I say to him through the chatter of my teeth. "Let's fuck shit up!"

He thrusts his arm up into the air and appears to jump, but leaves his feet on the ground. "Fuck it up!"

"I need an arrow!" Yardstick yells. "Gonna shoot you, witches! Whoa!"

I laugh. The Cuban laughs. There is only silence and darkness from within the lavender eyesore. From the car, a blond girl, Yardstick's most recent chick, brings him a handful of arrows. She looks a little scared, but joins in the festivities anyway. Intelligence is not her strong suit, but she is kind, and smoking hot. She's a white-trash kind of pretty with awesome curves and very low morals.

"Fuck cunts!" she yells. "We are going to Wizard of Oz your faces!"

"Tell 'em, baby," Yardstick says, closing his eyes, trying not to laugh. He almost drops the arrows, but maintains his composure enough to gather them for the blast. He appears anointed with the role, the ecstasy careens through his body like an homage to some screwed-up god of war. "Take these."

She reaches out and grabs all but one of the heavy-tip bolts. The brightly colored shafts have a large four-pronged arrowhead at one end, and two-tone feathers at the other. These arrows are made for hunting, just not this kind.

Yardstick loads the crossbow with ease. "Here it comes, witches!" he yells, right before he takes aims.

This house is in our crosshairs a lot. We have come to spread the word here three times in the last eight days. We visit with rocks, beer cans, sticks, and obscenities, all hurled from the safety of darkness. In the daylight, we drive by honking and waving. We have never seen the occupants. The witches give us stories for our drinking games, but they are not the only stories we tell, nor is this the only place we use the crossbow.

Four-way stop signs are our preferred destination. We pull up and wait for another car to approach and stop from a different direction. At that point, the kid in the passenger side of our vehicle leaps out, brandishing the weapon. I am amazed at the speed at which someone ducks when motivated by fear. Most people retreat under the steering column with the appearance of one of us holding the handcrafted purple-hearted beast. After we fire the projectile at the vehicle, the fascinating part is the amount of time that passes before the chosen ones stick his or her heads back above the dashboard. We stand at intersections for as many as five or seven minutes, waiting to get our rocks off on a stranger's fear of the unknown. When they come back to the surface, we cheer for them, as if they have been reborn, as if this is a baptism for their personal growth, as if we are the righteous hand of America's future. We do not think we are causing serious harm.

Yardstick studied the matter in great depth. The arrows have different-sized tips; the small ones deflect off the windshield with only a small chip to the glass, the largest four-pronged heads will blow through a passenger door (not the glass, the actual metal door) and come halfway out the other side. We save the large ones for car dealerships and expensive houses. To those in our aim, the size of the arrow does not matter. Each one is big enough to kill a man.

"Give it to them, baby!" the blond girl screams.

Yardstick pulls the trigger. The releasing of the bolt is noisy, like the metallic clank of an aluminum bat on a garbage dumpster. It's not quite as loud or scary as a gun, yet still very effective. Yardstick's aim is right on line, but the arrow ricochets off the iron bars of the door and flies off into a dark corner of the yard. The street is a rattle of sharp sounds, then silent.

"Mow your fucking lawn, assholes!" Yardstick shouts, grasping for another arrow. "I want my fucking arrow back!"

The Cuban and I scream and applaud, drowning in the rhythm of the roll, searching for something to throw.

I NEVITABLE
1988

I SIGN MY NAME ON THE PIECE OF PAPER. A man in a white nurse's uniform leads me away from the admittance desk where my mother sits, tan and joyful, with her new boyfriend, looking as if all this is normal. She doesn't say goodbye. I look at her over my shoulder as the nurse and I amble away from her. She smiles. We turn the corner; I still feel my mother sitting in that room draped on Bob's arm. I know she can trace my unseen footsteps in her mind as I walk through the back hallways of the hospital's main building—she was committed here last year.

That is why I am in this fucking place.

We pass by another hallway, the nurse motions with his arm, pointing lazily to the art and physical therapy rooms. The sterile shine of wax on the floor reflects the hush lights. A solemn energy pours in from the window at the end of the hall. The corridor has a ghostly glow. The furniture of the offices, the art on the walls, little spurts of carpet, and the expressions on the faces of the employees are framed in neutral colors. The fourth door we pass catches his gaze.

The nurse, in no real hurry, stops to chat with someone out of my sight line; my mind races, imagining where the exits are located. My whole life is in this small zippered duffel bag resting on my knee: a toothbrush, underwear, socks, shorts, T-shirts, a thesaurus, and folded notebook paper scribbled with poems. I could flee this place and just disappear. I remember the gas station down the street at the corner, got plenty of smokes but no cash.

Call collect.

I formulate the conversation with my cousin Craig in my head. His words are always the voice of sweet reason and he would urge me to stay. Besides, he is still asleep, he will not answer.

I have been down this hall before.

On a night just under a year ago, I walked down this very corridor, dumbfounded by the selfishness of my mother. "My mom is an inconsistent bitch," I say out loud.

We make another turn toward a large double door with glass windows facing another set of identical doors. Beyond them is a courtyard. My time to shine, I imagine pulling an O.J. Simpson as the door opens. I see myself hurdling the benches and bushes along the concrete path of the courtyard, vanishing into the brush and out into this part of North Dallas. I remember Medical City Hospital is just around the corner. The air-conditioned towers would be a great place to hide and wait for a ride.

We cross the second threshold, stepping into the radiance of the July midmorning sun. The humidity is surreal, a deafening heat. Everything is a sticky blur, as if a bomb of sunshine has exploded in front of us on the sidewalk. We stagger from the blast, pausing to look for a few seconds at our surroundings. The nurse acts like a tour guide, pointing out the dining hall and gymnasium. To the left are two youth and three adult houses.

"The youth and adults never mix," he says sternly.

I think of my former stepdad Steve and his exit from our lives without a goodbye. He is eight years younger than my mom and ten years older than I. When I was thirteen, he was a twenty-three-year-old mix of adult and youth, already married to my mom. The first night they met, they picked me up from the skating rink in his Mustang. We went to the video arcade until they closed at two in the morning, then the drive-through at McDonald's. He was just another one of the men my mom met at a bar, but that first night he took time to impress me and not seduce my mom.

Two months later, after he moved into the apartment with us, that all changed. I always looked at him as more of a big brother—a brother who banged my mom, as loud as he could, and every chance he got. He tried to build a bond with me but we never sustained a connection. He wanted children and I did not count.

Last year, the day after my mom was committed here, I called to tell him my car broke down. He asked where it was and I told him. Since I was still his stepson, he helped me get it home and fix it. When I walked home from school the next day, I found my car stereo and a note on the dining room table. The car was his. We have not spoken since.

Just another man my mom met at bar and fucked.

"AU-1," the nurse says as we approach two metal doors with a keypad entry to the right. Lost in my resentments, I have forgotten about making a break for it. I turn to look back at the courtyard. The sun is still blinding, even behind a squint. In the two hundred feet we walked, my shirt has melted to my body.

After my mother got out of here, she moved to Florida, no longer feeling saddled with raising a boy, her life finally lived for her own ends.

She sure seemed happy.

So the past year, I walked as if amid the aftermath of an earthquake. I was not sure how to find myself in the rubble of my mother's life and the half-built temples of my own. At this moment, I am convinced that her relentless pursuit of everything but motherhood is to blame for my shortcomings.

While all the kids I went to school with prepare for college, I still do not have my diploma. Instead, I prepare to walk across the stage of a loony bin.

"Here we go," says the nurse, then he pauses.

The door opens. A slingshot of cool air pelts my sternum. I move forward, drawn into the confines of a refreshing darkness.

FUCKING CRAZY PEOPLE
1988

I SCAN MY SURROUNDINGS OF CLOSED BEDROOM DOORS. When I arrived on unit, they told me to expect a quiet day. I am the only one awake and there are just three others. The nurses' station is within earshot of my half-opened door. I hear them talking about a disorganized nurse who leaves discarded snack wrappers and crumbs all over the counters. The nurses sound like old women playing cards at the Sunday church potluck. They giggle with frowns.

I sit on my bed and stare into a prefabricated jungle of hunter-green lounge chairs and love seat–sized sofas. The community area is walled with foliage of real trees in big green planters surrounded by lush fake bushes of varied sizes. These separate the living area, the smokers' table, and the ping-pong table at the far back of the L-shaped room. Conversation pits of four chairs and a coffee table are scattered throughout with giant growths of underbrush trapped below the high canopy of the jungle trees. It almost seems real except for the absence of tropical birds. An enclosed courtyard allows natural sunlight to flood the walls. The warm beams full of dust flakes pour into my room. I watch tiny particles fall over the bed and off its side, slowly sliding to the surface of the floor. The hours of silence watching the shadows crawl and listening to the swirl from the air-conditioning vents across the landscape of the loony bin takes its toll on me.

What the fuck am I doing here?

Bored beyond measure, I have no desire to leave the safety of my room. The urge to run is futile. I am stuck here for two weeks. Eighteen years old and tired of my life, I have no home, no direction to run, and no plan for the future. I have been running my whole life. My legs are heavy from tireless sprints trying to keep up with my mother and her instability, with my father whenever he finds it convenient, and into any perversion that allows me to fill the knot of my guts with pleasure: dope, sex, destruction. The ramshackle love of my parents' marriage taught me how to tamp emotions down, holding on for unavoidable explosions. I accept the conclusion that living with my crazy mother has made me crazy.

Every half hour someone sticks their head in the room to ask if I am all right.

Dumb people ask the stupidest questions.

I no longer have the ability to lock my own door.

This place sucks.

I perceive Green Oaks to be a haven for people who drool on themselves.

Maybe they will give me some Valium and let me pass the time in bed.

The idea of mingling with crazies turns my stomach. I can barely stand to be around my mother for ten or twenty minutes, let alone a psych ward full of insane mothers. This pushes me over the edge.

The other bed in my room is empty. I remember the crazed and fucked-up folks my mom was housed with, their eyes never really connecting to you, except out of desperation to seem normal. An arm's-length hello is all I am willing to give them.

I do not want to share this room with a douche bag. Some happily married father of three who leads a secret life—sucking dick in the porn stores. Worse than a faggot; he is a liar to himself, his wife, and most importantly his kids. Probably fucks them too. Faggots and pedophiles never cure.

Fear of the unknown makes me rigid.

The cotton blanket becomes an irritant, steamy and rough. My fingers feel worn threads balled up at the frayed corners. I imagine how the clumps of cotton lengthened and tightened over the strange bodies underneath them through the years. I imagine the door revolving like the inside of a jet engine, ejecting the cured while injecting the insane.

There is a youth unit connected to this one by a long hallway and four sets of metal and glass doors. Two L-shapes square the enclosed garden. At least there will be people my own age.

Why did they not place me on that one?

Over the years, my mom's shrink, Dr. Judy, became like a family friend. She let me ride in her Jag the day Steve and my mom married. She has big blue eyes and blond hair, kind of a mean broad. She never fell for my bullshit. I used to sit on her couch with large pillows over my lap and shoot my mom and Dr. Judy the bird behind a pleasant smile. At age eight, ten, and twelve, I did not want to go to therapy. I did not care to hear about the feelings of my unstable mom. Dr. Judy informed me that if I did not quit flipping her off she was going to come over and break my fingers. Dr. Judy is coming first thing Monday morning. I feel like she fucked me over and I do not want to see her.

"I shouldn't be here," I say aloud, lifting myself off the bed. "Fucking crazy-ass mother and her selfish bullshit." A resentful loneliness flows over me. "Why did she do this to me? What the fuck is her problem? Crazy-ass bitch." My voice escalates. "This ain't fair, fucking bullshit assholes!" I can hear my words out beyond my door, bouncing off the large round columns of the community space.

I grow irritated by the lack of activity. I grab my smokes

from my bag and make a decision to keep my mouth shut. If you open your mouth, lie. My life is my business. I saw what probing minds did to my mother, wrecking her confidence and wholeness. No matter how many friends in their twenties she had in Florida, no matter how blond her hair turned under the heavy radiance of the sun, no matter how big of a smile medication put on her face, I knew the unhappy truth about her. No one is going to know that about me.

I approach the nurses' station. A black man in a polo shirt doing paperwork doesn't notice me. On the left of the station, next to the door, hangs a large board. Names written in blue and red are aligned along the left. The right side is lined with columns indicating patient statuses, their level on the unit, if they are actually on the unit or not, and any special instructions. My name, freshly written in blue marker, does not have a number and a letter rank. My status listed as *New*, it states that I am on the unit, and the special instructions read, *Suicide watch*.

"I need a light," I demand. "Not to kill myself with." I chuckle, now understanding why they took my belt, shoelaces, razors, and lighter.

"No, you need to ask politely if you want to smoke," the man responds, not looking up from his paperwork. "And life ain't fair."

"Life is as fair as you make it. Can I smoke?"

"You don't believe that now, do you? If you did, you would not be yelling at yourself, alone in your room. And the proper question is, *Please, can I smoke, sir?*" He glances up at the board reading my name. "Mr., ah, Mr. Carney." He looks directly into my eyes. "We learn to do things the correct way on this unit. Would you like to try again?" Somewhere in his mind, he knows exactly what I am thinking.

Fuck you, asshole.

"May I please have a light so that I may please smoke a cigarette?"

"*Sir,*" he states.

I huff, "Pretty please, sir."

"Sure, here's a lighter. Return it after you light your cigarette, sir," he responds. I am unsure of what he does around here. He is dressed differently than the nurses. His smile is full of concern. "You may smoke over at that table, sir."

"Thanks," I say.

"Thank you, sir."

"Thank you, sir."

The smokers' table is a long, rectangular folding table. Smudges of ash and rings of coffee cups adorn its surface. Every bit of edge is crowded awkwardly with folding chairs. They look mangled, as some of the cushions are torn and picked at like scabs. There is a deck of cards, most of which are worn and creased. A score pad and pencil indicate Spades is the game of choice.

The way the nurse called me *sir* intrigued me. No one has ever addressed me in that way. Never been anyone folks would want to call sir. I only call my papaw and my grandfather sir. The word seems appropriate for men of their ages, not for a young guy like me.

"Sir, you did not return my lighter," he states, sitting down directly across from me. "My name is Eric, I am one of the weekend counselors." I hand him the lighter and he pulls a Kool from his pocket. "Going to take some time, but you'll figure it out."

"Figure what out?"

"The routine, takes a little time. Most folks are shell-shocked upon admittance. After three days, they let you go to the cafeteria, if you are not a behavioral issue. Then you receive a rank on the board and they assign various therapies to fill your day. The process just takes some time."

"Where is everyone else at?"

"Either on day pass or on the field trip," he says. "You

learn the routine, and after a couple of months they might let you go on one."

"I don't plan on being here that long, a few days tops. No need to learn the routine."

"Huh," he says, as he inhales a long slow drag of the menthol.

"Once they see I ain't crazy I am gone," I boast, taking my own deep drag. "I start college in the fall. Got to be in Florida by the end of August."

His eyes study me in a peculiar way. Almost as if he is just watching me watch him, learning my reactions to his movements and inflections. "What school?"

"Florida State University in Gainesville."

"Good school." He smirks. "I thought you had to finish high school before you got into college." He looks down at his hands, then up at my face. He knows he has caught me. A slow drag, a slight hint of satisfaction expands in his cheeks. "FSU is in Tallahassee, Florida, not Gainesville," he adds.

"I'm not stupid. I just finished summer school. I'll have a diploma in my hand soon." My knuckles tighten and pale, a harsh pink blotched with white.

"Looks like you and I will be spending time together." Smoke escapes his mouth as he crushes the cigarette in the crowded ashtray.

"I doubt it, probably be gone by next weekend. I am not crazy."

"You like playing games?" he asks, walking toward the exit to the adjoining adult unit. "I like playing games. We are gonna have plenty of time to play some games together, Mr. Carney."

"You think?" I say, folding my arms.

"Don't play games with yourself. All your thinking brought you to me." He again focuses directly into my sight. "Three days will go quick. The board games are in the cabinets under the television. Pick out your favorite and we will play on Sunday morning. I hope you're a better cheat than you are a liar."

MY CAR IS A TORTOISE AS I TURN ONTO ABSHIRE STREET. A paper towel from the convenience store is pressed against my bad eye, sunglasses holding the towel in place. The sun parades across the concrete. My eye is killing me. C sits on his front steps, impatience on his face. As I pull up to the curb, he swaggers over to the passenger door.

"Can you take me to Jack in the Box, J?" he asks, already buckling his seat belt.

He looks fresh. Clean clothes, a shower, a crisp new hat sits on his head sideways. I look like *Night of the Living Dead*. We have both had the same amount of sleep.

"Damn, J, you look like shit. What's up with the paper towel on your eye?"

I remove my sunglasses and carefully peel the wet towel off my face. Irritated and red, the eye stings as it catches the light. My face clenches as if a long needle goes through my eye and into my brain.

"Damn, your eye is fucked up, J. That shit must hurt. Let's go to the Box."

"Sure. Not a problem."

This will not take long.

"Get some Visine for that shit. See a doctor. Get some sleep. Something." He laughs.

My breakfast decision made for me, I pull away from his house. I hate these little errands, side trips that distract me from entering and leaving this neighborhood as quickly as possible. Most of the times I roll through here, my mind is on a glass ship orbiting some distant rock in the blackness of his pocket. There is a panic to the journeys. I am always tweaking for more.

"You need to quit smoking this shit. Crack is fucking you up," he says.

"Why don't you quit selling it to me?"

"J, you know that you are gonna buy it. I know you are gonna buy it. You know I know you're gonna buy it. Why would I let someone else make money? I need it."

He looks at me as if deliberating over something deep and spiritual. I am too high and exhausted to know. He is correct. If I did not come here, he would not sell to me.

"I only have a few fifties this morning. Have to go re-up," he says.

He throws four on the middle console. My right arm jumps to grab the packages while I peer in the rearview, paranoid the cops are behind me. Watching. There are no cops. The street is quiet. I stuff the bags into my pocket.

"Heard you got pulled over by the po-po last night," C says.

"Asked me what I was doing out here. Gave me a warning."

"Glad I wasn't in the car."

"You're not kidding."

"What did you tell them?"

"Told them my cousin Viv is a street walker over here, that I was looking for her. She really is. That's the funny part."

We pull into the Box, a long line of cars waits for the drive-through. I look out at Buckner in the rearview mirror. The street bustles with commuters heading toward the highway, throngs of buses crowd at the bus stop across the street. The line inches forward. We don't say a word.

My leg bounces, I'm anxious to smoke the rocks in my

pocket. I am anxious about having the dope in the car, having him in my car, the fact I can barely lift my head to look where I am going. I am anxious about the sun and the piercing pain I cannot escape, about my unknown destination today. I grab the water bottle from the cup holder. I hang a fresh towel and the bottle out the window and soak down the brown paper until water runs from the edges. I slap the towel to my eye.

The moistness eases the dry skin of my eyelid. Slowly, the irritation fades, leaving a calm sensation on my face for a minute. Then the dryness returns. We pull forward in line.

"Four tacos and a Jumbo Jack," I order.

I hand C the bag, he pulls out his burger and tacos. Leaves mine in the bag. Déjà vu. I pull out onto Buckner, signal flashing against the heat of the morning. He hands me the bag, I fish out a taco.

"Can't believe that shit. They let you go with that dumbass story without searching you?"

"I know. Crazy, huh?"

I make the right onto C's street. He laughs as I pull up to the curb in front of his house.

"That is some white-boy shit right there," he says. "That shit would never happen for a nigga like me."

"You're probably right, I got real lucky."

"Shit. Luck ain't got nothing to do with it." He smiles. "All right, J, hit me up later, I will have more. Take care of that eye."

"All right."

"Be expecting your call around one, one thirty," he says, shutting the door.

"We'll see."

"Yeah, you need to get some sleep. That eye is fucked up."

I pull away from the curb, simultaneously unwrapping

the taco. The stale shell is almost too hot to hold. I bite down. The tops of my gums sink into the cheesy grease. I do not notice the taste.

NORMAL
1988

"ALL IN," THE ATTENDANT SAYS, reading the sign-in board. "Everyone's back in from breakfast.

"Group's in thirty minutes!" the attendant yells over the squawk box.

"Mr. Carney," the other attendant at the nurses' station addresses me quietly, "there are some new patients on the unit this morning. You have a roommate. He requires privacy this morning. Don't enter your room. Give him some space until dinner."

I have to stay out of my own room?

All the others head to their rooms to get ready for the day. I do not.

Fuck the new dude.

I turn to walk away, unhappy.

"Thank you, sir, for understanding," he says.

"Whatever," I mutter.

I walk to the card table. As I pass my room, the door is closed. I stop. The suspense of not knowing kills me. Ten inches of space separates my hand and the knob. I pause. I focus my energy on the door. I strain my ears. I can't hear anything, except the voice of my own fear.

Why is that fool crowding my shit? What is his problem? Hope he is not a suicidal freak. Cross-dressing sadist. Schizophrenic babbler. Alcoholic dad who beats on his wife. Fucking loser.

"Mr. Carney," the attendant reminds me.

I head to the card table, pissed I'm barred from my room, my bath.

Motherfucker better not have taken my bed or looked through my shit.

As an only child, I have never been good at sharing. My things were always mine. Assuring a safe place for my belongings became a ritual because nothing was ever permanent. They never stayed long. Boxed and shuffled again, my possessions, like friendships, shed every year or two.

My time here has been bearable because I can escape to the privacy of my room. Alone, I write my poems and read my thesaurus. Since last fall, I carry that reference book everywhere. One of my teachers, Mrs. Edwards, stapled together a manila folder to organize my poems. That folder and the thesaurus are all I ever take to my classes.

No poems today.

Now some unknown dude occupies my sanctuary.

He is a cutter. A bed wetter.

The unit has a few of those already. In my mind, they are the dumbest and weakest on the unit. I remove a square from the pack as I approach the table, cursing under my breath. There is a new man at the table. I act as if I do not notice.

I take a chair across from Terri, a cutter. She is a very good-looking girl with short brown hair, highlights, and blue eyes. In her midtwenties, she looks like a teenager. She is tall and thin; soft shoulders lead to the full roundness of her breasts. They brush against the length of her arms, as she raises and lowers her smoke. She normally wears long-sleeved shirts and complains that it is cold. We all know she is hiding the scars. Today, she is wearing a muscle shirt and Calvin Klein pajama pants. From the bend of the arm where junkies find Jesus to the end of her wrist, she started her own kind of search.

Long scars running various directions and sizes mark her

flesh. Abrasions flicker in the light of the room, revealing the acts of a frustrated girl lost somewhere in transparent rage. There is a distance behind her, as if conversation requires too much effort or is not as entertaining as what goes on in her mind.

She is fucked up more than most of us.

She avoids my eye contact. I spend my time admiring almost everything but her face.

"What's going on, Terri?" I ask. I like her.

"This is Flat Top, he's new," Debbie says from the table. One of two women with the same name on the unit, we call her Debbie. The other we call Deborah. They both annoy me like my mother. Debbie is overweight with every known affliction. Her nose turns up at the end like a pig; when she eats, it grosses me out.

Why do I have to stay out of my room if he is at the smokers' table?

I run my gaze over him nonchalantly, while my mind picks him apart. A sense of excitement flows inside me. This dude appears to be sane and respectable.

"I can tell that he's new," I respond. "My name is Jason, welcome to paradise."

"Thanks," he says in a cordial, nonapprehensive tone.

Early twenties, twenty-two, twenty-three, maybe.

He seems well put together—a short buzz haircut, tan, lean, not muscular but rather defined and toned. You can tell he exercises.

I think I made a big deal out of nothing.

Silently, I study him for a minute, listening to the conversation I interrupted. His eyes connect coherently with the person who is talking. He does not twitch like some of the patients, doped up beyond measure.

He is normal. I lucked out.

"Where you from?" I ask him.

"Bedford."

"Where are you from?" Flat Top asks.

"Mesquite, mainly. I moved around a lot. Go to college?"

"I finished a couple of years ago; I'm an accountant." He smiles.

"What kind of music you into?"

"I don't know, all kinds, I guess." He makes eye contact, winks, and looks at Debbie. "So Debbie, you were saying . . . ?"

That was kind of weird, but friendly.

"Friday is movie night. After dinner, we pop popcorn and pile around the television. Saturday nights tend to be quiet, depending on how many weekend passes are given out—"

"Saturday night sucks," I interject. "Flat Top, you're close to my age. We should hang out; play ping-pong or a board game."

"Not really, I'm twenty-seven. But maybe we can play sometime," he says.

He doesn't appear to be that old. He wears a nice button-down shirt and Levi's. The scruff on his face is barely visible.

I bet he's a Republican and a Baptist.

His body language suggests manners and comfort in social situations.

This guy probably never been in a fight but I bet his word is very solid.

There is no wedding ring on his hand.

Probably got a hot girlfriend, having a college degree and a good job.

He appears mentally stable.

What the fuck is wrong with him?

"Oh, that isn't much older," I say, looking for a friendship starter.

I want a roommate I can trust, smart and witty, a new best friend. The smokers' table ours to rule over, our jokes playing off one another, forcing everyone to keep up. Unlike now, where Phil, the dickhead that he is, sits in roost.

Phil is middle-aged and we clash. Acceptance is important to me. Moving as much as we did, I am eager to fit in. Sometimes I am unaware of how socially awkward I am. Terri looks at me, knowing my motives. She smiles a wicked grin, gives reassurance to my actions.

"You do drugs?" I inquire.

"No drugs. I used to drink." He smirks again. "What are the groups like, Phil?" He avoids me once more.

"Well, since you don't do drugs, if they give you sleeping pills, let me have them," I say.

"I don't take sleeping pills. You wouldn't like the medications I take."

"Antidepressants, huh," I say. "That's cool."

I do not care what they are, as long as I can get high. So far, I have not found any support in my medicinal inquiries. Most everyone here likes what he or she takes.

"Something like that," he says. "You wouldn't like them."

"The therapies depend on your physician," Phil explains. "They prescribe your course of treatment. Some of us do more than others."

Phil is a know-all, like my dad. He says things like, "You sure you want to smoke, Jason? You sure that's the best use of your time? How is throwing balls of paper into the basket therapeutic? Is singing out loud with headphones on considerate?"

I dislike Phil and his stupid questions. In his midforties, married with a few kids, whom he never talks about, his hairline fights its extinction with sporadic long strands combed over the gleam on the oily globe of his head. He sits in his chair at the smokers' table and ponders with great affect the situation of others. Observing him reflect on your illness—large hairy hand rubbing his cheek and chin as he draws in a deep breath and waits for a long pause to develop before enlightening everyone around—is like listening to Gandhi discuss the nuances of human equality. I have no idea what is wrong with him and guess it has something to do with thinking he is more doctor than patient.

Most of the patients have the same couple of doctors: a sand nigger (Phil's), a fat woman, or Dr. Multiple Personality. They are on the unit most of the day. Gone at dinnertime, so I haven't seen them on the unit past dark. I am Dr. Judy's only patient on the unit. They all seem on track to fulfill their release dates. They work treatment plans laid out in careful measure by their doctors. Nine days and I have not spoken with Dr. Judy. She came on unit *once*. Signed my release from suicide watch, wrote my treatment plan at the nurses' station, and smiled at me across the room. No time to talk to me, she has patients on the other unit waiting. Instead, I have lots of group therapy.

"Group therapy sucks," I enlighten everyone. "They told me that you would be fragile, some kind of snot-blower. You don't seem fucked up at all."

"Now that isn't very supportive, Jason," Debbie snorts. "We need to build a safe space here."

"It's a compliment," I respond. "He doesn't look fucked up. Are you fucked up?"

Terri giggles. I interpret this wrong and flash my winning smile at her, as if the hook-up is on. Flat Top just puzzles at me. Phil stares down at the floor. Debbie smacks her moist jowls, her thick tongue resting on her lower lip. There is an uncomfortable silence. I do not understand what is wrong with what I said.

How is the truth a bad thing?

"When I came in, I didn't talk to anyone. Didn't want to." I clear my throat. "All I'm saying is that you seem well-adjusted and comfortable for someone in our situation, thus not fucked up. So, what the hell is wrong with you?"

"Jesus, Jason," Phil says.

"Jason, really now," Debbie snaps. "You need to think of how other people feel."

I stare at her. "How is your daughter doing today, Deb?" I question. "Hope y'all are finding some clarity?"

Terri giggles under her breath, sweeping at my leg with her foot, under the table.

Debbie's daughter is on the youth unit connected to this one. We all know this because she talks endlessly about how they are going to rebuild their life together.

Horseshit. She fucked up her daughter so bad you can tell the teenage girl has had enough of this bitch.

I understand her daughter's pain for two reasons: I have a fucked-up mother named Debbie and I hate sessions of group therapy with Debbie; she never stops talking.

"She's doing great. I got to visit with her over the weekend; we were both out on a pass," she says, missing my sarcasm.

I ignore her. "No, what I am trying to say is that if I am getting a new roommate, I am relieved that you're not fucked up in the head or something."

He smiles. "Well, I am fucked in the head, but I'm rooming with Phil."

"Oh?" I say, surprised. "I just assumed you were my new roommate."

All the effort I've just put in, for nothing. The fear of the unknown drifts back across the sun-filled room. I stare at my door. Serene quiet flows over the frame; something occurs to me.

Why is this fucker not on suicide watch? Why does he get to close the fucking door? I hate this prick.

"I came in with your roommate. He is really having a hard time today." There is a concern in his voice, compassion.

Kind of feminine.

"Just what I need, a whack job," I say.

I want to take a shower and brush my teeth.

"Jason, please stop," Debbie says to me. Then she addresses Flat Top: "I hate to pry but what is wrong with him? You know, so we can be more respectful of his situation."

She is judging her sickness against everyone else's. As if to her, there is some kind of medal or trophy for being the craziest person in the mental hospital.

"He looked physically sick," Flat Top responds. "They said he has some real problems. I heard something about domestic violence issues."

"That's horrible," Debbie exclaims in that fake kind of way. "When my ex-husband beat me my world fell apart. I developed an eating disorder. I think that's when my daughter became bipolar."

"Your husband beat you?" I say.

I feel a little guilty about the way I treat her. No matter how much she gets on my nerves, I would light her husband on fire if I caught him beating her. I do not tolerate men hitting women.

Tell the court my father made me do it.

"I'm not sharing a room with a man who beats his wife. That is some bullshit, fucking cocksucker."

"Wow, don't hold back," Terri says. "Good for you, express yourself, take a stand for your principles." She rolls her eyes.

"Jason, you don't know the specifics. Would it not be reasonable that someone could change?" Phil asks.

"Thanks, Phil," I say.

Would it not be reasonable that you are a fucking bleeding-heart-liberal douche?

"I put up with it for a couple of years, right up until the divorce, even once after. I'm going to talk about it today in group. I'm having some issues now," Debbie says.

"Great, Debbie. You have to work through that," Terri says quietly. "We're getting so much accomplished."

Terri, without notice of the others, makes a motion of slitting her wrists. I smile at her, nodding. Every morning at nine, every afternoon at one, and then at four o'clock is group therapy. Most people on the unit have two a day. I attend all three, speechless. We sit in a circle, and stare at one another.

Very healing.

The therapist asks if anyone has any issues. Then we probe the depths of that issue to a resolution of some sort and move on to the next person.

A bunch of bullshit.

Debbie always discusses issues. When the group finds resolution and moves on, she brings the conversation back to herself. If you do not ever want to talk, throw it to Debbie.

"What kind of man beats his wife?" I know the answer to this question. I fear my father sleeping one bed away in the dark of my room.

"Who said he beat up his wife?" Flat Top asks.

"You did. You said there were some domestic violence issues."

"Well, he was the one being abused, so . . ."

"What kind of man gets beat up by a woman?" I say.

That is so much worse.

"All kinds of men suffer abuse at the hands of dominant women. In our society's estimate it is approximately—" Phil starts.

"If you don't like it, don't let her tie you up, Phil," I snap.

You ass-fuck douche bag.

"His boyfriend hits him," Flat Top finishes.

"Oh my," says Debbie.

"He's a faggot?" I am stunned. My flesh glows white, like an affliction.

"All right, young man, would the way you're conducting yourself be offensive to those around you? Are your terse comments and mannerisms the most effective way of communicating with other people?" Phil glares at me.

"*Terse?* What the fuck does that mean? Fuck you, Phil." I stand. "Would the way you annoy the fuck out of me be something I should kick your ass for? What are you upset about, got a queer brother? Douche bag," I steam. "You're a faggot too, Phil. Bald-ass, know-it-all cocksucker. You talk to me like that again and I'll kick your ass." I pick up the pack of cards and hurl them into his chest.

"This is so therapeutic and we're not even in group yet," Terri says, laughing nervously.

The eyes of everyone at the table are on me. I don't move, just stand there fuming. Disbelief hovers on their faces, as if none of them approves. Phil stands after a moment of deep thought, anger all over his face. The way he marches to the nurses' stand resembles a five-year-old.

You must be shitting me, that tattle-tale bitch. The shock of the situation freezes my face; I am terrified of queers. *I am not rooming with a kid-fucking faggot.*

"I am not rooming with a fag."

"Homosexual," Terri says.

I imagine his lecherous fag lips caressing my body as I sleep, when I change clothes, in the shower. A wave of disgust runs up my spine. A dirty and familiar feeling courses through my veins—the same as when I was a little boy terrified of bathrooms. Bathrooms felt alone and dark; outside the door, I tingled, unable to move. The urine a warm sensation running down my leg. I never understood this fear, and I still do not.

Ain't putting up with no gays.

"Jason, I'm sure he is a nice man," Terri says, looking off into the corner.

"Then you room with him. This ain't fair, I should get a say. Put him in a room by himself."

"Why?" Flat Top asks.

"Cause the gays are perverts." I stand firm. "That is why all those fags die. Their sins are being judged."

"That is ignorant," Flat Top says, tears now in his eyes. "You're lost."

"Ever read the Bible? Ain't no salvation for a sodomite. And I ain't sharing a room with one."

The attendants start to walk over to the table escorted by Phil. I catch them out of the corner of my eye. "Fuck you, Phil. You fucking pussy." I know what is coming.

"Well, you got a faggot for a roommate," Flat Top smiles through his anger. "One with AIDS too."

I hesitate. The way tears pour out of his eyes and venom out of his mouth reminds me of a frail teenage girl who just got her heart broken for the first time. Shocked by the totality of what he just said, and his full-blown emotional response to it, my fear consumes me. A feeling of dread hangs over me. There is no hiding my emotion. The fight gone out of me, I feel like a little boy alone in the dark. The bathroom comes back.

He is going to try to rape me. I feel tears building behind my own eyes. *These motherfuckers are out to get me.* My thoughts make no sense. *I am going catch AIDS.* I first learned of the virus in 1984, when it hit Los Angeles, where we lived. I was sure the world was coming to an end. *He is going to infect me.*

"They fucked me, I should have gotten the normal roommate. You should have been my roommate," I say, turning my fear to anger.

"Who me? The normal roommate?"

"Compared to the queer with AIDS, yes," I say. "I don't care what your problems are, you're not a faggot with buttrammer's disease." Tears flow through my anger. Everything is crashing in around me.

"Mr. Carney," one of the attendants says, placing his hand on my shoulder, "let's go."

"Jason, I am here because I want to kill myself," Flat Top says, somber and under control.

"I could live with that. That's my mom's deal," I say, laughing to calm the friction, as the attendant pulls me from my chair. Another attendant grabs my arms.

"And just so you know, I'm also gay."

I stare at Flat Top over my shoulder as they lead me away, his eyes pink and swollen with tears.

Wow, you look so fucking normal.

CORNERED
1988

THE ROOM IS A SMALL OFFICE with a table and three chairs. A narrow hall off the nurses' station leads to three doors and the trio of rooms are exact replicas. On the white walls hang framed prints, none of which go together to form any sort of theme. The scene of the English foxhunt matted in hunter green and framed in cherrywood catches my eye. A large pack of dogs corners the fox in the hollow of an overturned tree. The gnarling hounds' faces beckon to their masters. The hunters are mounted on fine steeds, their coats the color of blood and their faces shining with prosperity. One cradles a bugle to his mouth. I can almost feel the blast of the instrument; its call echoes through the tall dark verdure of the forest.

The air conditioner blares through the vent. The room is frigid. My shorts and T-shirt are not enough to keep warm and I tighten up like a snake in my seat. All the light in the room is artificial, there are no windows. The door contains a large square of glass, with chicken wire floating inside to discourage thoughts of breaking it. Two potted plants, both covered in dust, one a large tree, the other a medium-sized bush, stand facing each other in opposite corners. They resemble two over-the-hill fighters as they square off and await the bell.

"What are we going to do with you?" Dr. Judy surges

into the room. Hands full of files and a large briefcase slung over her shoulder. She throws her belongings on the table, peers around the room as if she forgot something. Her glasses dangle at the end of her nose; her designer suit is wrinkled. She looks like a mad scientist. Her presence fills the room.

"What are we going to do with you?" she asks again, opening the door. She steps into the hallway and moves into the kitchen. She takes her time. A nurse stops in the doorway to the kitchen and asks her a question. I hear my name. Dr. Judy says something and they laugh.

That bitch is laughing at me.

There is a coffee cup in her hand. Her rose-colored lips cool the top of the cup as she saunters back into the office. As she opens the door, she says, "Well, don't keep me waiting."

"Let me leave," I respond, not making eye contact.

"Do you really think that's going to happen? How long have you known me?" she asks as she sits across from me.

"Why am I on the adult unit?"

"Jason, you're eighteen, all of your actions from this point forward in your life will be judged as an adult," she states sternly. "You keep playing around and they will put your ass in prison. Or you'll end up dead."

Her blue eyes always look directly at me when she really wants to make a point. She spends a minute staring into my eyes. She holds a large file in her hands. I can see my name written on top.

What the hell is in there?

All of our previous interactions have concerned my mother, and her inability to focus on life. Today, we focus just on me. It is the first time, and I have nowhere to hide. This makes me uncomfortable.

"Where have you been?" I ask.

"What happened today?" she counters. "I am not very happy about getting called away from the patient I was with."

"I got a queer roommate. He has AIDS. They made a mistake. You have to do something about this."

"I intend to. Now, what happened today?"

"Great! When do they move him out of my room?" I say with a smile.

"He will not be moving."

I think, *This is unfair, but if it means no cocksuckers then I am comfortable with moving.* "When do I get a new room?"

"You will not be changing locations either." She smiles. There is an arrogant twist to her lips, extended up in the motion of knowing something I do not.

"Then what are you going to do about this?"

"I intend to listen," she says in a matter-of-fact tone.

"How does that help me?"

You listened to my mother for a decade, and Mom is still crazy.

"You need to learn to talk about your emotions and feelings. To express yourself in constructive ways, which do not hurt those around you, Jason. What happened today?"

"Talking about a fag ain't going to remove the fag—"

"A gay man is not your problem," she interrupts. "Jason is your problem."

Fuck you, bitch.

The nerve of this know-it-all woman and her degree from Southern Methodist University. Mom has dreams of me attending SMU and graduating law school. Never happen. I am smart enough to do this, but I lack discipline. Dr. Judy is a lot like my mother, which pisses me off. Her tendency to dominate the situation, always asking questions to which she already knows the answer, annoys the shit out of me.

"So, where have you been? I have been waiting on you for over a week. When do I get out of here?"

"I have other patients. I think being stuck on this unit is good for you. You need to learn to interact positively with other people, you lack respect for the feelings and desires of others," she says, removing a yellow legal pad from her briefcase. "I'm not on your time frame, Jason." She uncaps a black ballpoint pen. "However, your release is totally determined by the progress you make. *You* determine when you go home." She slides the pen and legal pad over to me.

The pad is a familiar comfort. I have written poetry on yellow legal pads since I was a kid. I find a particular brilliance to black ink written on the yellow hue of the paper. The way I can look at the page and see the words aligned before I write them is the most healing feeling in my life. The only daydreams I seek are poems. Just having the pad within reach calms me.

"I get it: don't do drugs and be nice, keep my opinions to myself," I say. "Can I go home now?"

"Drugs aren't your problem; Jason is your problem." She removes a fancy pen from her jacket, starts to write in the file, not even looking up as she speaks. I try to peer over the top of the file as it dangles diagonally off the table, resting at the top of her lap. I can't see a thing.

"What home do you want to go to?" she asks. "The dysfunction of your grandparents' house or do you want to continue to chase your mommy?" She sips her coffee. "It's time to grow up, Jason."

I can feel color blooming across my face. Dr. Judy knows what buttons to push. I have no response. I tune her out. My grandparents' house, my choice, because I can flounder there doing whatever I feel like doing. I lived there the last couple of months of school. Laziness overcame my grandparents' good sense. This way life wore them down. After my aunt Barbra died, it became easier not to look. I have always avoided responsibility, always held the belief I can get my shit together tomorrow.

I sit in the chair stewing, no compromise in my gaze. I

know it is tomorrow already. Under the table, I shoot her the bird.

"I don't care if you like what I have to say or not," she says, finally looking up over her bifocals.

"I don't," I snap. "And I ain't sharing a room with no queer."

"I'm more concerned if he wants to share one with you," she snaps back. "This is how this is going to work. Like it or not. You will attend all of your groups. If you aren't contributing by the weekend, I'm dropping your level back down."

She continues to write in my file, her hurried scrawls scratching the paper. I really dread being stuck on the unit again, losing the freedom of going to the cafeteria.

"Whatever."

"If you have any further offensive outbursts, or show any further hostility to any of the other patients, you go to the safe room." Her finger points across the table like a gun. The one true thing about Dr. Judy is that she will not fuck around with you.

I have never seen anyone go into the safe room, but other patients talk of how they come inject you with a sedative, place you in a straitjacket, and stick you in this padded room at the back of the unit. They leave you there for at least a day, strapped to a buckle in the wall. Closed spaces make me very uncomfortable, as do large crowds.

I want no part of the safe room.

"I expect an apology from you to the offended parties on the unit, at dinner. If you don't do this you lose your privileges," she continues. "I'll be here to start your one-on-one session Monday morning, as long as you don't fuck up. I can outwait you. I have all the time in the world."

"Whatever," I shrug.

"*Whatever* isn't going very far anymore, mister," she says. "For the next two hours, you are going to stay in here. Use the pad and pen to make a list of ten things you hate about homosexuals. Then write down why you feel that way. Share what you've written in group. You have until the end of the week." She starts to arrange her files, closes her briefcase. "There is a colleague of mine coming in the morning, to administer some tests. I expect you to be civil and respectful to her. Answer the questions honestly. You only hurt yourself if you continue bullshitting your way through life, Jason."

"Whatever." I blow her off in my mind, lost in the scene of the foxhunt again. The serene stare of the fox, teeth bared though he is surrounded, grabs me.

"You start participating in group therapy and I'll assign you to different therapies that aren't on the unit," she says, opening the door. "If you don't start working, you'll find the next four to six months goes by slower than you can imagine." She shuts the door, walks away.

Four to six months, she must be out of her fucking mind.

I stare at the legal pad and dream poems about elegant hunts for smart-ass doctors.

Passive
1980

I SIT IN THE OFFICE, on a large expensive couch, bored out of my mind. I cover my torso and lap with the plush green pillows.

My mom pays too much for this shit.

Glass windows line the far wall. I stare out at the pale blue sky, listening for the sound of the traffic ten floors below. I can hear only the annoying voices of my mom and her doctor. Her shrink, to be more precise. She says the experience of talking with someone about your problems leads to a more fulfilled existence. From what I have seen, these sessions lead only to more self-doubt and a dependence on someone else's opinions.

"Deborah, how are the writing exercises coming along?" Dr. Judy asks.

"I enjoy the affirmations, do them every morning," my mom answers with a smile.

Bullshit! I have seen her write her affirmations, but only when her boyfriend and she get into a fight: *You are a strong person. You are a strong person. You are a strong person.*

What a load.

Dr. Judy is headstrong. She intimidates my mother, which is not easy. My mother runs under a full head of steam most days, yet around Dr. Judy she tends to be meek. A well-educated woman, Judy Cook is a single mother and very attractive. She has stunning blond hair. Several years older than my mom, Dr. Judy is the kind of woman that my mom dreams of becoming. I do like her, but do not like being in these sessions. What fourth grader would?

"How are the headaches, Jason?" she asks me.

"What?" I say, wondering, *What she is talking about?*

"The headaches? You've been going to the nurse's office every day complaining about severe headaches, your mother tells me." She stares at me, wanting an answer. "She even said you went to Dr. Muncy, who prescribed you Tylenol 3 with codeine. Why would you give a nine-year-old codeine?" she says, glancing at my mom.

"They come and go," I answer, face hidden behind a pillow.

"Tell me about these headaches; how often do you get them?"

I say nothing. The floor-to-ceiling bookshelf behind Dr. Judy's desk intrigues me.

So much knowledge crammed onto those shelves. You have to be really smart to read all of those. Mostly medical texts, there are a few novels and some biographies. I love biographies. History has always caught me, mainly because remembering things is so easy.

"Well, what part of your head hurts when you get these headaches?"

"I don't know."

"Don't know?"

"I can't remember. Have you read all those books?"

My mother bites her fingernails. She seems unsure of where all this is going. I'm not. This is an ambush. Dr. Judy, with all her ornately framed degrees on the wall, does not ask stupid questions. My mother doesn't realize she is closing in for the kill. I hate coming here. The conversation always shifts to me, as if I am willingly going to participate in this absurdity. I don't need a shrink. I need a mother who is stable and sane.

"The nurse called your mother last week," Dr. Judy tries to get my attention. "She told your mother that you have taken most of the bottle at school. That you come in complaining midmorning, take a pill, then nap for a couple of hours. She doesn't believe your head hurts at all."

I don't say anything. Under the pillows, I flip her off with both hands. My fingers lock in place with the ferocity of a Doberman grabbing a piece of meat.

Fuck you and your degrees.

"Quite frankly, I don't think your head hurts either," she adds.

"We're worried about you, Jason," my mom says. "If there is anything you want to talk about, this is a safe place to do it. I love you, sweetie, how can we make you better?"

Make yourself better.

I see my mom as weak sometimes, cowering around the fragility of her scars. We all have scars. Some of us did not ask for them. My red face clinches, swells like a man playing a trumpet. The bird is still waving off my hands.

"Debbie, don't baby him," Dr. Judy responds. "Well, mister, what do you have to say about this? There is obviously a problem. You tell us what's eating at you."

My mom's suicide attempts my family calls accidental. My father, who I have not seen in two or three years, has a new family. Another new school; I've moved five times in the past year. The bad dreams at night I do not understand. The kids who beat me up at recess after lunch. My mother goes out more than she stays home. Her boyfriend, who treats her as an afterthought. The frogs I kill with firecrackers at the creek. Sneaking out of the house at night and stealing money from my mom and her roommate. I love the way the pills make me feel just before I fall asleep.

I click my shoes together in frustration. I cannot think of a way to get out of this conversation. My resentments jumble; I don't know where to begin.

How can my mother do this to me? If she would have just said something to me, I could have lied and we both would have felt better.

I scan the top of the shelves for something to catch my attention; a bottle of aspirin is out of place on the third shelf. The brown-and-gold label is half torn, as if someone got anxious.

"I'm getting a headache. Can I go to the bathroom?" I ask.

S O CLOSE
1988

THE FAG ROOMMATE does not know I am in the room. I cannot take my eyes off him. He faces the far wall, asleep. I absorb the stench of his slumber. His ease and comfort irritate me.

Why should this faggot get to rest?

His exhales invade my space. Rough streams of air gurgle over the mucus lodged in his throat. I am uncomfortable in this situation.

Sick-ass homo.

The seven feet between us might as well be seven inches. Seventy yards would be enough to ease my mind. I can smell him; baby powder and vapor rub intermingle in a pasty concoction. I have not seen his face, just a small glimpse of the back of his head. Long yellow stands of hair string out of the top of his blanket, shimmering in the half-light from the bathroom. I imagine him as the foulest creature. His eyes beady slits, his hands claws, not fingers, his yellow nails filed to knife points. I imagine they puncture and hold me in place while he sucks the life out of me. There must be rancid sores, coarse hair, and scabs all over his body.

Something horrible is going to happen.

I lie flat on my bed, expecting him to levitate out of his sleep and lunge at my bare skin. I tense up like an animal afraid of something bigger out in the darkness. The same fear falls over me that held me against the wall in the porn store. I flinch with thoughts of the man in green, the secret of his sandpaper tongue and the abrasions it left on me. My skin crawls.

He does not move.

Can I catch this shit by breathing his tainted air?

I pull the covers up to my nose and tuck the blankets under every square inch of me. A cotton and polyester fortress, a moat of white sheet stretched along the mattress surrounds the walls of my paranoia. I breathe into the covers. I do not feel safe.

Self-pity consumes me. The man in the green shirt had eyes so much like my father's. I do not understand why I am comparing them. I feel trapped. In this room, in this hospital, in my life a constant whirl of wrong choices.

I don't care anymore.

My arms pressed against my sides, I am stiff as a corpse under the sheet, locked inside a morgue's freezer. I am too scared to take my gaze away from him.

This is not a fair punishment.

His back is to me, the mound of his body resembles a small woman. His feet shuffle under the sheet; the wrinkles of fabric snag and pull against his toenails. A hiss across the threads.

I catch myself in drifts. I feel like everything is on top of me. Too much to handle at one time, I know I belong in this place, though I will not admit it. I don't know consciously why. An answer that I seek to a question I do not yet know I am going to ask lurks under my skin. There is something about him, his close proximity to me, the fear of the man in green, abstract thoughts of my father convulsing in my muscles; I get scared that it's all interconnected. My life in shambles, I do not understand how I am to pick up the pieces and move on.

Why am I surrounded with this sickness?

I reach for the yellow pad on the nightstand. These are the first words I write about faggots: *Someone slides his hands under the darkness, laughs in lustful ways.*

I stare at the ceiling and wait. The lights will come on at six; I only have four hours left.

THE NIGHT IS STILL. The air outside my window feels like the end of June more than the start of April. I carve through the current of warm air. My car hurls over the asphalt in a spasm of fiberglass and steel, driving unmanned toward East Dallas. I am a blank daydream humming in unison with the song blaring over the radio. I care for the safety of no one, not even myself. The orange buzz of the streetlights floats above the highway. Without thinking, I change lanes into the exit. The ramp pours onto the service road, curves around a tree line. The orange lights above drown in the white haze of the car dealership at the stop sign. I turn right onto Buckner.

Buckner runs four lanes in each direction, from one side of Interstate 30 to Ferguson Road. For as far as the eye can see on the other side are crack-house apartments. Decent hard-working neighborhoods trapped in the shade of the complexes. The innocent bystanders who own houses and raise families on these streets are engulfed in warfare, not of their making. Because they are poor. Congested with traffic on foot and wheels, from sunup to sunup, this street holds darkness like a desperate con.

I do not need crack.

Why am I here?

I don't know the answer. The truth is that I just need to talk with someone. I decide to pull over at the gas station to buy a drink.

People trade themselves at discounted rates to find crack's

exhilaration. When the sun goes down, the gas station is a hustler's paradise. The usual gaggles of folks mingle in the parking lot: panhandlers who ask me for me change as I exit, the homeless crackheads who offer to pump my gas and wash my windshield for a couple of bucks, and a loud woman weighing less than her lost teeth who asks if she can suck me off out back. The middlemen smokers, who detest any form of work, try to separate me from my money with offers of straight drop—the best dope. They never have any drugs. They take victims down the street and disappear into the darkness with the funds. Gas station dwellers are an army of half-dead zombies conjuring rocks from coins. I am quickly finding my place among them.

"What's up, J?" Easy asks. "Let me pump your gas. I got a card."

I've known Easy for a while now. He was the only witness to a wreck I had on Thanksgiving. A car made an illegal turn, all five of the occupants said the accident was my fault. Only Eric said anything different. He stuck around to make sure he was on the police report. Every time I see him, I try to help him and his wife with a couple of bucks, a ride, or a pack of smokes. Little things to me are large gifts to him.

"Sounds good, let's do twenty."

This is a common hustle, popular among intermediaries. The person with the stolen or borrowed credit card offers to buy gas at discounted rates. I hand Easy the cash, make my way inside looking over the parking lot.

I buy three packs of smokes to go with the six I have, an orange juice, a Coke, and a bottle of vitamin water. I am not that thirsty. Walking back to the car, I notice a couple in the shadow of the trees along the sidewalk. There's something familiar about them. I look up and they are gone. I do not give them a second thought.

"Thanks," I say to Easy, handing him a five for his troubles.

"You need to score tonight, J?"

"No thanks, I got it."

"Let me hold a smoke," he says.

I hand him one of the packs in my hand. "Where's your wife at?"

"She's around someplace. You know us, we always getting our hustle on." He reaches out to shake my hand, his next customer in sight already. "Be good."

"Y'all be safe tonight," I say, climbing back into my vehicle.

I head out of the parking lot back toward the highway. As I reach the first stop sign on the bridge, perspiration seeps out of my hairline, the craving for a hit comes over me. There are slabs in my room. I decide to run by C's house anyway.

You can never have too much.

I turn at the entrance ramp and head back the way I came. Something off to the left catches my eye. Eerie whispers run through my head, up my spine. A man and a woman covered in dirty moonlight walk under the bridge. I decide to turn around at the second stop sign. It is the same couple from the gas station. They move in and out of the darkness with a constant ease. Their movements look familiar. I do another U-turn to pull up behind them. I met them before.

The girl approached me the other night, getting gas. I was less than thrilled about talking with her since I thought she was going to offer sex. She only wanted to bum a smoke. I gave her a few and said good night. The way she walked away from my kindness was heartbreaking.

I roll down the passenger window as I come up behind them. "Y'all need a ride?"

They look at each other, never saying a word. They climb in, she in the back, him up front. We pull forward. No one says a word. I flip a U, head over the bridge down the long stretch of Buckner away from C's house. I plan to hold them hostage with crack. They can smoke my dope free of charge, as long as they are good company. I hope their plans are no more sinister than my own. I look into the rearview, the girl is hard to find, small, sunken into the backseat.

"What y'all out doing?" I ask.

"Getting our hustle on," the man says. "Do you need to score?"

I laugh. When you smoke crack, you learn early on that intermediaries are never a good thing. Do not buy crack from people who smoke the stuff as well. They will fuck you. Your twenty-dollar rock becomes ten. Most times, what you get is crumbled leftovers of what they impatiently shoved into their stem as they made their slow way back to your car. Your money feeds someone else's addiction while yours starves.

"I got the hookup, thanks anyway."

"All right," he says. "I got the straight drop."

I do not respond. The girl squirms in the backseat. She huffs with disgust at my refusal of their offer. Crackheads wear emotions on their sleeves. I can tell her energy level depends on how close she is to the next hit. I totally understand this sickness. She obviously thinks I have motives other than smoking dope. She sinks further down into the shadows of the backseat.

"Where we headed?" The pickup puzzles him.

"This dealer I know," I answer.

Not my regular dealer. I did not want to expose my regular connection. As we head the quarter-mile down the street, he counts the number of places where we could have scored. I turn in at number six.

"They got good dope here," he smiles.

The truth is that most of the dope comes from the same two or three sources along this boulevard. Every package is virtually the same. The only difference is the size. Dealers around here are like oxygen. They compete ferociously for business. This helps if you are a loyal customer as the packages tend to be larger with consistent purchases.

"Y'all wait here," I say, removing the keys from the ignition. "Be back in a couple of minutes."

From where I stand in the dark cavernous entryway of my secondary connection's apartment, I can see my car. Catch traces of the figure in the cab, the wash of a streetlight falling over the dark shadow of their ghostly skin. A shake pulses up my leg. A feeling of calamity shackles my mind. I have never picked up strangers before. An overwhelming urge to flee fills me.

Run! Leave those panhandlers, the crackhouses, and this insanity I smoke.

I begin to feel light-headed.

Breathe. They are not going to hurt you. Breathe.

I cannot stop, no matter how much I want to.

Breathe.

Marooned in my sickness, I want to run. I lack the strength. The sudden creak of the door jolts me.

"What the fuck do you want?" the omnipotent voice from inside barks.

I score two twenty-five-dollar solids.

Driving. They do not know what is going on. Their silence says everything. I keep looking in the rearview mirror. The girl keeps moving out of my line of sight, as if my eyes can burn her flesh. She is very young.

The dope in my hand makes me anxious. From the moment I receive the package, to the moment when the flame melts the rock, I panic for a hit or try to control it. I am tweaking in front of strangers, making it harder to hide. I constantly swivel around as if I have missed my exit. I do not know how to explain the voices in my head. The man keeps looking at the dope in my right hand. His tongue runs along the edges of his lips.

They understand.

"Do y'all have a place to stay?" I ask.

He shakes his head.

"Y'all want to come to my room and get high?" I ask, as if any crack fiend would ever decline free hits. "I'm staying two exits down the highway, over in Mesquite."

"That's where we're from," he says.

The girl does not say a word.

POETRY, SAID PATRICK
1988

"CAN I SIT HERE?" my faggot roommate asks. "You were very brave today."

I'm not brave. The muscles in my arms are rigid and snake-bitten. The legal pad bends under the force of my erratic scribbles. My insides are a pretzel. I am so full of emotions that the act of crying is painful. I keep writing, don't answer.

"Debbie is not mad. She understands what just happened was about you," Patrick says as he sits in the chair next to me. "Jason, you really need to start talking about your feelings."

When is my fucking life not going to be about feelings?

The group therapy sessions are finally getting to me. My outer shell is cracking like a Jordan almond in the hands of a five-year-old. The daily onslaught of the staff's emotionless smiles, the vain attempts of the therapists to lead our discovery of the insides of our bowels, and the medicated grimace of the patients' secrets and fears on full display, the horror of it all has worn me down. I have nowhere to hide from my loneliness anymore. Debbie's story sent me over the edge. One second I was staring at my fingernails, the next is a blur.

"Leaving her daughter with that man makes her sadness seem empty," I say. "If she really loved me, then she wouldn't have left me there."

"Left *you* there?" Patrick replies. "You are transferring. Do you know what that is?"

"No."

"Haven't you been paying attention in group?" He laughs. "That's when you project your feelings onto someone else. That's what you just did. Why would you feel so strongly about *her* daughter's sexual abuse?"

I do not answer. I don't know. At least I will not admit the truth to myself. I stare at the yellow pad in my hands. Drops of tears cover the page. The page wrinkles in small circles, the blue lines of the paper are faintly fuzzy as they smear under the weight of my hand when I wipe off the droplets.

"I don't know where that came from. I feel bad for being so mean to her," I say.

Patrick reaches out and touches my arm. His kindness to me over the past few weeks has taken me by surprise. He is always in a good mood, always has a story or anecdote. He shares his snacks, never folds under the pressure of his illness. His strength is immeasurable, even more so when he shares with the group.

"I was supposed to share this in group today. My doctor said I have to speak up or lose my privileges," I explain.

"Oh, you did share," he says. "I think everyone felt you today."

I nod, making abstract patterns on the corners of the page.

"You like writing a lot."

"I guess. Poems."

"Who would have thought you like poetry? Can I read them?"

"No, it's not important," I say.

"I hear you up at night, writing. Hear you reading the words aloud as you write them. I don't understand most of it, but it sounds good."

I can feel him smiling at me, I do not respond.

They sound good is the typical response I get from my

family, when I read them my poetry. I resent the answer even though I very rarely offer them a poem to read, preferring that the words come from me.

"That's what you're writing at night, isn't it?" he asks. "About what? What are your themes?"

What does he mean about themes?

I never consider my subject when I start writing, I just write. Writing is a kind of disassociation, a tapping into what I call imagination, letting go to where I just allow the words and form to flow out of me. The poems start out elusive and contain little meaning to anyone other than myself. The act of writing is the only time I trust myself.

"Some," I say, "some are this affirmation bullshit my doctor has me doing."

"I hate those things," he says as he fixes his legs Indian style in the chair.

"I do too. My mother has been writing them for over a decade," I scoff. "They're useless."

"Not really, there's a lot of power in redefining yourself through writing affirmations. I just hate writing, not one of my strong suits."

I look up, intrigued by his statement. My hand relaxes on the pen and something very true connects inside my body.

"How so?" I ask.

"Affirmations are a visualization of what you would like to become," Patrick states, sounding more like a therapist than a patient should. "What do you want to become? If you think about it, poems are affirmations."

"I guess, but I don't really think about what I am writing, I just write. Had a teacher tell me to edit my work and understand my emotional content to enhance reader experience or some bullshit. I just write."

A couple of months ago, one of my teachers took time to

ask about a poem I spent a month writing instead of paying attention in my classes. I think some of my teachers were just happy I was not a noisy distraction during algebra, geometry, English, and French, so they did not say anything about it. I must have changed each word four or five times, more so in the sheer enjoyment of using my new thesaurus than anything else. The poem was far beyond dark and cryptic; my English teacher read the long-winded megasyllable wreck once—she asked if anything was wrong in my life. Clueless.

The teacher that I had for advanced reading, an honors course (the only one I ever qualified for due to a lucky score on a standardized test), invested in me; she took time to question each line, to show me how to ask the right questions when editing; how each line pertains to not only the poem as a whole, but also to each line surrounding that line, most importantly every line's relationship to itself. I am not that evolved yet as a poet to understand this. I paid as much attention to her as I did the clueless one. She tried to tell me that through editing, a poet can create a more concrete piece. I was more enlightened to know there are eighty-eight different words I can use for *run*.

"You just write. No reason? No purpose?"

"I guess. Sometimes."

"Do you write about yourself?" Patrick asks.

"I don't know. Maybe."

"What are your affirmations about?"

"I'm lonely. I'm angry. I'm lost. I'm a thief. I'm tired."

"Not very positive." He laughs. "They're supposed to be what you want for yourself."

"If I have to share them, I would rather they be short and to the point."

"What do you mean?" he asks.

"I sat in my doctor's office on that plush couch listening to my mom sob while she affirmed herself to the doctor's approval. Every statement long and drawn out. They would spend an hour and only cover one or two things. The whole thing was very sad. The less I write, the less the doctor has to talk about and the less time I have to be there."

"You're not showing them to the doctor, you're showing them to yourself. By writing affirmations, you're giving yourself permission to heal. Isn't it about knowing who you are, writing for you, defining the world you live in so that you have a better understanding? I mean, fuck everybody else."

He sits back, his body full of grace and fluidity. Almost regal without effort, his smile exudes more confidence than my whole body has ever known.

"Dude." I pause, stuck with the strength of his statement. I have never thought of writing like that before—just for me, not for a reader or audience.

"Why do you write poems?"

"I don't know," I say. "I like poems."

"But why write them?"

"I guess I'm good at it. Never thought about it."

Deep thoughts or examinations of life are not too viable for me. Most of my life has been about keeping up appearances while hanging off the edge of a cliff; any attempts to stop and examine the color or meaning or the scenery might have led to a devastating free fall.

"You have to define your love of something to truly know why or how deeply you love that person or thing, right?"

"I guess . . ."

"The words you write are from you and for you. A conversation with yourself can be the most freeing of experiences."

"Yeah, but what I am writing now is not for me. My doctor told me to write it."

"What is it?"

"A list," I say.

"Like a grocery list . . . ?" He laughs.

"The ten reasons I don't like homosexuals." I feel uncomfortable saying this to him.

"See how much progress you've made? A few weeks ago I was just a faggot." He laughs again.

"I have to share this with the group."

"Can I read it then?" he asks. "Maybe I can help you understand what you've written."

I never allow anyone to read my yellow pads. *My handwriting is rushed and in many cases hard to decipher.* That's the excuse I used to dismiss the attempts by my family and friends to show interest in my legal pads' contents. I look into his face and find only kindness—almost motherly is his expression. He removes the yellow notepad from my hand without any effort. He begins to read.

As he studies the list, he lifts his head a couple of times and smiles a somewhat confused smile. My fingernails pry in and out of my clenched teeth, I try to pretend I don't care. I do not take my eyes off of him.

"You have ten things here, Jason. Ten things you don't like about homosexuality. Is that correct?"

"Yes," I say, ashamed that these are my true feelings.

"Number four: *Slapping myself in the face when I feel gay after I jack off?*" he questions.

I explain. As an eleven-year-old I would stay home from school and masturbate nine or ten times during the course of the day. Before I could even ejaculate, each euphoric release brought forth the burden of humiliation from inside. Each time I tried to beat the pain of it out of me.

His face puckers with sadness. "That isn't homosexuality."

"What is it then?"

"Jason, what I feel for men is no different from what you feel for your girlfriend," he says. "Being gay is not about sex—well, it's about sex a little—but more importantly, being gay is a way of describing an emotional attachment to people of the same sex."

"So am I gay?" I ask. This fear has consumed me most of my life.

"Are you attracted to men?"

"No, of course not."

"I don't think you're gay. I have seen how you interact with women. You are definitely a straight boy."

"Why do I feel so gay after I jack off?"

"How does that feel, when you're done?"

"I don't know . . ."

"Yes, you do, just think about it. You've got the answers."

We sit in silence for a minute or so, our eyes connecting and glancing away.

"Well, what is the first word you think of?"

"*Ashamed*." I mutter. "*Dirty*. You know, *wrong, gross*."

"Being gay isn't feeling dirty," he says. "And it's definitely not wrong. Jason, when I read the list I think you're talking about incest. Has someone hurt you?"

I do not say anything. He knows the answer, even though I don't.

"Number six: *Green shirt, glasses, and a chick with a dick*." He smirks.

"That was me hurting someone else."

"Number nine: *The blind girl in second grade, and my fantasies of having a sleepover with her*."

"I don't want to talk about that."

"Do you think it's an accident that you're here?" Patrick asks.

"No," I say. "I belong in here."

"You're very lucky. Most people don't get this chance to start over, especially at such an early age."

"Lucky? I don't feel lucky. I feel like I'm crazy."

"Well, you probably are, but not incurable. You're not as

tainted as you think you are. I see hope inside of you."

A little feeling of peace begins to spread in my belly. For the first time in years, I do not feel like I am consuming myself with each breath I take. The way he is talking about me is full of hope, a hope I have never given to myself, a flicker of possibility that makes this place seem like it can be a distant memory someday.

"You've been wasting time in here. They won't let you go home until you start to show progress. How can you do that?"

"I don't know," I say.

"That's bullshit, you do too."

He sounds a lot like my doctor. I roll my eyes. Now I just want these feelings to go away. All my life, I have understood that if I do not look at how I feel then I do not have to worry about it.

"Do me a favor, write about this: write about your life through poems. You can change your world if you just write about it. You have a really neat gift; believe in it."

"I feel crazy writing about all of this," I say.

"This isn't going to be easy. However, I promise if you write down what you feel, it will get out of your head. You'll see your feelings clearer; have a better understanding of who you are."

"Where do I start?"

"Start with number one. When you finish, go to number two. Just think about what you are writing as you write it. Give it purpose. Each word you write is a piece of insanity that you are bringing into the light. Each word makes you free."

"Okay, I can do that."

"Pinky swear," he says, holding out his little finger.

"You're such a fag," I reply with a smile, wrapping my finger around his.

"Yes, I am, but you're not." He smiles back. "You're just bat-shit crazy."

"Right."

"Jason, you don't see this yet. Your strength is in your poems."

Half As Dirty, Twice As Smart
1988

I STARE INTO THE TOILET BOWL. The contrast of the stark white porcelain, the clear sparkling water, and the delicate nature of the cotton swab, submerged at the bottom of the toilet, heightens my fear of the bright orange-yellow disease stuck to the swab's bulbous end.

What the hell is that?

The bathroom carries the feel of sudden illness, the air around me congested with invisible germs.

I know I'm going to get sick.

The runny scrambled eggs and coffee from breakfast bubble in my stomach.

What the hell is that? Did that come out of his ass? That is so fucking gross.

My eyes scour every surface—the tile, the sink, the shower floor, my towel on the rack, and the sides of the commode—searching for more signs of this Day-Glo funk. In my mind, I am convinced there is AIDS at the end of the Q-tip.

He is going to make me sick.

Although rooming together for two weeks, I still feel uncomfortable. Everyone else seems to like Patrick; he tells funny stories. They don't seem bothered by his gayness or his sickness. I smile and try to play along. His honesty has made him a dependable member of the unit's community. He doesn't struggle when talking about how he feels in group therapy. There is a softness about him: his body gestures as he converses with the other patients, the constancy with which his eyes connect to the person who is talking, and the hugs he offers when they finish sharing their pain. He would never hurt anyone. From what I gather, other people have hurt him a lot; his last boyfriend was very abusive. Patrick reminds me of my mother. Most of the time he shares in the group sessions, I try to ignore what he says. I can handle feeling only so much compassion for fag shit.

"What are you doing?" Patrick asks. "You drop something down there?"

I do my best to ignore him. *I should've closed the bathroom door.*

"Let me brush my teeth real quick," he says. "Scoot."

Before I can say no, he comes over with his toothbrush in hand. There is not much room for more than one person in here. I back up to give him space. Patrick turns on the water and begins to apply the toothpaste. His straight blond hair hangs over his forehead. I can't see his eyes. From the back, he looks very much like a petite woman—a small delicate frame and fine, shoulder-length hair. I watch him comb the tresses at night, right before lights-out. He reminds me of my cousin Jill as a child, practicing to be pretty. The way he studies himself in the mirror, checking for imperfections in his skin, resembles a teenage girl. He primps quite often. Even the way he holds one side of his hair back as he brushes his teeth is feminine.

My eyes keep going from the toilet bowl to him and back. To my thinking, even his toothbrush and hairbrush are covered in that sickness. I keep all my toiletries in my shaving kit, in my dresser. I want to say something about his unsanitary behavior, how his careless disregard endangers me.

"What are you doing?" he asks with a mouth full of minty foam.

Startled, I do not know what to say. "Nothing."

He gives me a quizzical look, then goes back to brushing. I glance back at the toilet. The thick orange clump at the end of the Q-tip pulses like a beacon from the depths.

I have to say something.

"What are you staring at?" he asks, peering at me in the reflection of the mirror.

"AIDS," I mumble without thinking.

"Huh?"

"You can't leave that there," I say.

He pauses there with a look of confusion on his face. Toothpaste runs down the sides of his mouth. I gesture with my arm to the bowl. He questions me with his eyes. I watch the droplets of his toothpaste-saliva drip into the sink basin.

This whole place is contaminated.

"I don't want to get sick," I say. "You have to flush that shit."

He looks into the bowl and then at me. His face contorts, his nose wrinkles like a bunny, his finely tweezed eyebrows scowl, making him look like a scorned woman. He bends back into the sink and rinses out his mouth.

"I don't know what you have to do to take care of yourself. Whatever . . ." I hesitate as I search for the words, trying to avoid an unpleasant confrontation; the topic makes me very uncomfortable. I'm unable to stop grimacing at the way he spits openly into the sink. I'm barely eighteen; I never thought I would be having this conversation. "But when you're done putting stuff up there, be cool and flush it."

"Flush what? Up where? Explain what you are saying. I don't think I get it."

"You know when you're done cleaning . . . the . . . you know . . . the stuff—"

"What stuff?" he interrupts.

"That stuff, you know . . ."

"Know what? Spell it out."

"The stuff . . . you know . . . the AIDS out of your butt in the mornings—get rid of it. Spray Lysol on the toilet and sink, be considerate of others, man." I'm not sure if that came out right, but I feel lighter now that I said it.

"You're kidding, right?" He looks into the toilet. "So, you think the orange stuff on the Q-tip is AIDS from my ass?" He stares at me for a few seconds. "I would be really pissed off if you weren't so fucking stupid." He laughs in a condescending tone.

I'm confused. The grin on his face grows ear to ear.

"You're shitting me, right?" he says as he turns to leave the bathroom. "Hold on." I can hear him mumble to himself in the other room.

"What are you doing?"

He returns with a Q-tip in his hands. "You ever use one of these?"

"No," I shake my head.

"You're tragic," he says. "Hold still."

I freeze, unsure what he is doing. He grabs my chin with his left hand, jabs the cotton swab into my ear with his right. There is a good amount of pressure within my ear canal as he twirls the shaft. I flinch from the uncomfortable sensations of his touch and the sound of the cotton cleaning my ear. He pulls the bulbous end out.

"Well, look at that," he says, holding the Q-tip in front of my face.

The fluffy cotton is matted and clumped; it is caked up with so much orange wax, the end appears an earthy brown. The sight is disgusting. He throws the swab into the toilet with the other one. I stare down watching it float to the bottom, where it rests on the other Q-tip that looks half as dirty. I am amazed.

Earwax, Jason you're a dumb-ass.

"You better go to the doctor," he says with a chuckle. "Looks like your ass is in your ears."

TRIPLE-D COKE CANS
1988

"WHAT ARE YOU DOING?" Patrick asks.

"Getting ready to talk with my friend over there," I say, pointing in the direction of the adolescent unit on the other side of the building. "My doctor told me to write down some points that I want to discuss. His doctor, he, and I are having a powwow tomorrow."

"Must be hard having a friend your age so close, but unable to hang out," he says with a smile. "Is it hard being with all us older folks?"

"I sold him drugs. He's kind of gay. We were not really friends." I pause. "And I wish I had more in common with y'all sometimes."

"What do you mean, *kind of gay*? He wouldn't be a faggot to you?"

"I don't know. He just hung out with some dudes I assumed were gay. I shouldn't call people names. I guess I should apologize for that."

Where I went to high school in Mesquite, any boy who was different was a fag. When boys fought in the halls or the parking lots, varied homosexual slurs were always the insults of choice. *Dicksucker* is probably the most offensive thing anyone can be called. I've used this language since I was five. I learned *gaywad* and *gayrod* as derogatory terms before I knew what being gay actually meant. Those terms and others like them are part of the vocabulary of being a straight white boy in Texas. *Gay* means something that is retarded and dumb, in addition to the obvious meaning.

"You're making progress," he says. "So you hung out and did drugs with these guys you thought were gay."

"No. Sold him drugs. Sold lots of kids in my school drugs. Even the star football player, who drove a black Corvette, bought for him by his dad. That prick would never talk to me except in passing to try to score some weed. Didn't make us friends."

"Oh," Patrick says, staring at Michelle and Mark. They are sitting in a conversation pit on the other side of the communal area.

"Same thing with this guy on the teen unit, he would call me for coke or speed and nothing else. That isn't friendship."

I continue writing on my yellow pad, the top two pages folded over the back. I don't know what awkward things I am supposed to say to this person. For the last hour, I have scribbled and crossed out fake sentiment after bullshit excuse. I feel that our doctors making us come together to seek resolution and support for one another is "gay."

"How did you know he was here?"

"What is going on over there?" I ask, noticing that he is focused on something on the other side of the room.

"Anticipating good news," he answers. "Go on. How did you know he was here? I'm listening."

"The other day I came back from getting some tests done. Y'all were still in group, so I was chilling out here by myself, when the entire teen unit strolled through."

"Did he say anything?" Patrick asks. "What did you do?"

"I didn't do anything, didn't recognize him at first. All the kids seemed to be staring at me, though; I guess he told them who I was already."

"Well don't let that bother you, be honest with him. Look

at all the positive experiences you're having," he says with a funny smile. "You never know how incredible a new connection could be."

He is being too coy.

I look to the other side of the room; Mark is talking with Michelle and smiling at Patrick. These two very different men seem to be playing some sort of game.

"What are y'all doing?" I ask.

"Being stupid," he says. "Why don't you tell me what you wrote? Hey, you're level 3B, right?"

"Yes. Why?"

"No reason. What are you going to say to that boy?"

Out of the corner of my eye, I catch him nodding his head to Mark.

They are up to something.

As of late, these two have shown real interest in me. Mark has been on the unit for a very eventful three weeks. He is the scariest person on the unit by far. He is very muscular, and when they brought him in it took three orderlies to hold him down so they could sedate him. He is not very tall, maybe five eight. His arms are extremely long; they look like they belong to a much taller man. Mark talks a lot about ghosts who haunt diners on the other side of town. I thought he was very cryptic, until I realized he did seventeen years in prison. I do not ask about the ghosts. When he mentions them, I cringe.

"I'll say sorry for selling him drugs, I guess. I don't know. Just going to see how it plays out."

Mark stands up and makes his way over to where we sit.

"Y'all going to be all right?" Patrick asks, seeing Mark approaching.

"Yeah, we're cool," I respond.

The other day in the gym, Mark and I had an altercation. I knew better than to argue with him, though I did not even have a chance. Mark acknowledged his mistake and I didn't get into any trouble. He is in his thirties, and extremely angry; has been most his life. I am not the only one who notices this fact. When the group therapy ends, you can tell when Mark shared. Often as his group exits, a look of horror is frozen on the faces of those who listened to him work through his insanity; some people are just sicker than others. Mark bears the prison mentality of *angriest man on the block wins*. In here, he wins.

"What are y'all doing?" Mark asks.

"Jason is getting ready to be confronted by his friend."

"Oh, that kid over there. Heard your doctor talking to the attendants about that," Mark says, sitting down in an open chair. "I wouldn't sweat that, he sounds like a pussy."

"Now that isn't very nice," Patrick says.

"Have you seen him?" Mark asks.

"No—" Patrick starts.

"Well, all right then, I trust what I heard," Mark laughs. "He's a pussy, just like Jason."

Mark winks at me. He is not wearing a shirt, hardly ever does. His torso is covered in tattoos—some big, some small, all look as if they came from a prison cell. On his face is a black teardrop at the corner of his eye. On his stomach, coming out of his waistband, is the outline of a .44 Magnum handgun. The tattoo gives the appearance that he is carrying a gun on his waist. He rubs at the handle frequently when he talks.

"You know I'm teasing, no hard feelings," he says. "Sorry for the other day. You're a 3B, right?"

I am smiling, not wanting to cause a problem.

"Yes, he is. I already checked," Patrick says.

"Why?" I ask.

The 3B level is the highest you can obtain on the unit. I have been at this level for two days. With this security clearance, I am allowed to venture unattended out to the court-

yard, go on overnight passes, and make runs to the soda machines on the other side of the courtyard every night at nine.
Because of this clearance, the attendants do not watch me too
closely. I worked hard the last month to gain this responsibility. I am making progress—3B means I am close to going
home.

"So it's on?" Patrick asks.

"She is if he is," Mark replies.

"Jason, we got a surprise for you," Patrick announces like
a proud older brother. "The good news—"

"Michelle is into you," Mark cuts in. "She wants to go get
soda with you tonight."

"Sure, I'll go," I say. I do not understand yet what they
mean.

"Dude, you're lucky," Mark says. "She's hot. You're going
to get some."

Michelle is very good-looking. She is tall. Around five
nine or five ten, long brown hair extending halfway down
her back. The bangs sprayed high, typical for a rocker girl in
the 1980s. Even though she dresses younger than her age, to
my eighteen-year-old thinking, she is all mature woman. She
has large, round, perky breasts that I stare at often. Her skin
is pale and freckles line the bridge of her nose, her lips are a
candy shade of red, even in the mornings. She is twenty-six
and married.

I met her husband when he came on visiting day. A nice
man with blond hair in his late twenties. He seemed very
blue-collar. Their conversation appeared to be forced and disconnected. They did not make a good pair.

"Yeah, right," I say.

"She said she's been flirting with you all week," Mark
elaborates. "She doesn't think you're into her, I told her you
were."

"Hell yeah," I say, still not sure if this is real.

"I told you," Patrick chimes in. "I knew he would go for it."

I still do not believe this is real. Mark is not a very trustworthy person. I can never tell what is a truth and what is extended. He has an angle. He has a scam—he trades and collects the other patients' medications for smokes or cash. Three times, I found him and Michelle's roommate hiding in the conversation pits, eyes barely open, sedated lumps giggling to each other. I think he is carrying on with her.

"I'm so excited for you," Patrick says. "You know there is a bathroom right next to the soda machines."

"You'll only have, maybe, twenty minutes tops," Mark adds. "Don't waste time."

He then looks over to Michelle and nods yes. She glances at me, smiles. I smile back, and give a small wave.

Holy shit. This is real.

She giggles and shakes her head in a good way. I am in her therapy group. I know very intimate details about her, especially about her relationship with her father; she knows very intimate things about me as well. We both have issues with sexuality. The muscles up my back tighten and tingle, my body builds with nervous anticipation.

I want to touch her boobs. Her enormous boobs.

I don't know what interests her about me. I do not care. I am here to get better, not to walk on water.

"We thought you could use some confidence," Patrick says. "You've been working hard, you deserve a reward."

"Or two," Mark chuckles, slapping me on the shoulder. "I bet you're worrying about a different pussy now."

WHAT IS NOT SAID IS IMPORTANT
1988

SUNDAY NIGHTS ARE SLOW. The weekends generally contain a lot of free time as a number of the higher-level patients receive day and night passes. Saturday and Sunday suck for socializing. Even though I am a 3B, I did not get a pass this weekend. My soda-run rendezvous attracted eyes of suspicion; my doctor thought it best if I stuck around. But my indiscretions are not at the forefront as the weekend closes. The unit strangely buzzes. Gossip lingers over the unit since yesterday when Patrick did not return from his overnight pass. We are all worried about him.

Mark and I play ping-pong in the far end of the communal area, mainly to get away from the gossip. Most of the other patients hover around the television or the smokers' table. They have decided that something horrific happened. Mark figures he went out with his friends and partied all night. I fear he could be hurt or sick. The orderlies and attendants group together at the nurses' station; they appear to be discussing some plan of action. Mark slams the ball past me.

"Pay attention. Pat's going to be fine. What are you doing?"

"Something is going on up there," I say.

"They're probably getting the meds ready. Get the ball."

As I start to serve, I notice two attendants exit the unit. Mark returns the serve. Something rare occurs—we volley.

Mark is tremendously skilled at the table. He is also good at dominoes, Spades, and basketball. All of these are activities one can master if one has a lot of free time.

"You're too good for me," I say as Mark scores again.

Most of the time we play this ridiculous game, I pick up the ball after he smashes the damn thing by me. The game becomes repetitive and boring rather quickly for me. I need some excitement. I pick up the ball again.

I decide I am going to serve from six feet behind my side of the table. I arch my body as if I am Jimmy Connors with a racket. My right arm throws the ball up in the air, as if I am on center court at the US Open. When I slam down, the ball rockets squarely into Mark's side. It bounces back onto the table, dribbles into a roll, and falls off the edge.

"What are you . . ." As I start to speak I notice he is not even paying attention.

Mark is focused on the door at the front of the unit. The two attendants have reentered, walking Patrick to his room. Patrick's face is swollen and pink. His eyes are puffy, as if he has been crying. The way he walks suggests he is trying to maintain some dignity. Some of the other patients leave their seats on the couches and the chairs of the smokers' table, heading toward him.

"They're letting me get some of my things," Patrick says.

He stops to hug a couple of the women, who reach him first. The attendants intercede and keep him moving forward. Mark and I start to walk over in the direction of the couches. When Patrick and the two attendants enter the room, the door stays open, though one of the attendants stands with his back to the communal area, blocking the view. They are in the room less than two minutes. Patrick exits carrying his belongings in an old suitcase and a white plastic bag.

"They're removing me because I didn't come back from pass," he says to Michelle as she hugs him.

"Goodbye, baby," she says.

"Take care, Patrick."

"Best of luck."

"We're going to miss you."

Patients reach out with their words and their arms. I stand at the back and do nothing.

The attendants keep him moving toward the door. I am about seven feet away from him as they reach the threshold. The rules prohibit patients from going to that side of the nurses' station; this is as close as I can get to him. While the attendant unlocks the door, he turns and waves goodbye to everyone. I want to call to him or raise my hand, but I do nothing. He waves at Mark, over to my left.

"See you, brother," Mark responds.

The door opens. A gush of air rushes past me as the pressurized seal of the unit breaks. I have goose bumps on my arms.

He does not see me. I am terrified. *I missed my chance to say goodbye.*

The three start to walk out.

Patrick stops—in an upbeat manner, as if he forgot something vital to where he is going—and turns around. He holds a couple of books, a bag, and a pair of flip-flops in his left arm. His face searches over the crowd. Once his eyes connect with mine, he smiles. Soft and whole. He lifts his right arm into the air, mimics the act of writing something. I nod my head, feeling this simple act with my heart. Then he blows me a kiss, turns back through the door, and is gone.

Everyone goes back to normal. The lock to the door seals the unit. I just stand there feeling robbed, still not sure what just happened; the whole event seems very surreal. Unprepared, I missed my opportunity to tell him so much.

I TOSS ONE OF THE TWO twenty-five-dollar pieces on the bed. Gather my pipe and the slab I have hidden in the night-stand. The panhandler girl's eyes light up, seeing the hundred-dollar hunk in my left hand as I remove the drug from the drawer. A strange concoction of excitement and fear bubbles over her. She almost cracks a smile; her face has the sinister quality of a young kid tearing apart dolls. I can tell she wants as much of this drug as I will give her, so much so that she will do whatever necessary to get her hands on it. The number of women who barter themselves for crack is staggering; the number of men who sell their wives and girlfriends for a few rocks is infuriating. I am not looking to barter.

"Have a seat. That one is yours," I say, pointing to the rock on the bed.

They say nothing. I walk around to the other side of the bed and sit in the recliner, next to the air-conditioning unit.

I ask, "Do y'all have a stem?"

I load my pipe waiting for an answer. They say nothing. Fear and excitement mix and bubble over me. I study their body movements for a clue. They both stare back. He is blank of emotion and energy. I am happy to have someone to talk with, but fearful that these two panhandlers might rob me. We exchange names. I quickly forget. The quiet of the room belies the voices in my head. Their ages stick better.

"Thirty-five. She's eighteen," he says.

"How long have y'all dated?"

"Two and a half years."

I thought about how old my parents were when they met. My father at twenty-four seduced a seventeen-year-old virgin, turned her into a mother.

Thirty-two when he teaches a fifteen-year-old about her body. What do her parents think?

I take a hit, believing him.

"Do you talk?" I ask the girl hiding behind her mess of dirty brown curls.

"Not when she's high," he answers for her.

The homeless eighteen-year-old studies the ground. She is small, no taller than five three and weighing not more than ninety-five pounds. Her hair is cleaner than the rest of her. Black soot cakes her long skinny fingers and hands. The dirt speaks of living in dumpsters, searching pay phones for coins, begging for change in gas station parking lots. They scavenge like birds. Large oily streaks across her skin show that she has not bathed in days.

The new dope tastes good. Not as potent as the larger slabs, but since I have been smoking the same stuff for days, the new dope has a different effect on my high. I place the large slab on the air conditioner unit just out of their sight. Tolerance levels build up quickly so changing flavors, so to speak, keeps the body guessing. My mind races.

He slides the chair away from the desk next to the nightstand. As he sits down, a brief look of levity rolls across his gaze. The muscles in his face relax. Close to a few hits, he looks almost human. He pulls out a thin metal tube, shiny like the outer casing of a fancy pen. Crackheads can make a pipe out of most anything. She sits on the bed next to him. Her knees are up so the soles of her shoes are flat on the white comforter.

I sit in amazement. He gives her the first hit off their pipe. It is rare among heads to control selfishness; it consumes the addict when the drug is near.

In some contorted, controlling way, he loves her.

Deep beyond the raging sickness seeping throughout his being, under all the scars built up over his thirty-five years, there is still a flicker of humanity lingering. To me it is an unforgivable sin to hand someone his or her first rockslide. There is no atonement for this; it is similar to taking something from little girls that they can never get back. So small and young, this girl must have been awkward, easy prey.

How old was she when he first hit her?

"Hey, I got some snacks here." I offer. "If you're hungry."

"Hell yeah," he says, grabbing a candy bar.

She smiles. Says nothing. He opens the wrapper with his hands, bites the metal tube steady between his lips. She ignites the lighter at the end of the pipe. He inhales as the wrapper falls away. He lowers the pipe, stuffs half the candy bar into his mouth. He chews feverishly; mouth open, caramel and chocolate melting together as he exhales his hit into the air. He is not timid.

"Pretty good dope," he says, clumps of candy stuck to his lips.

"Not bad," I say.

I notice the movie on the television is running through the credits. I explain the procedure for ordering another one. "If y'all don't want to watch porn, the channel list is on the dresser."

He orders more porn. She seems indifferent.

The stuff we are smoking disappears fast. I retrieve the hunk on the air conditioner. Break the slab into two pieces, hand the larger one to them. This gesture of kindness, as twisted as an act of kindness can be, causes them to look at each other oddly. As if they have been here before, the look in their eyes says, *When does this turn bad?*

C LAMOR
1989

WHEN I BOARD THE FLIGHT TO ST. LOUIS I have a bag, the promise of a new car, and the hope of a college education. I have no other options. This is the moment I've always pined for. My dad wants me. The eager enthusiasm with which he has approached this situation takes me by surprise and makes me question the haunting memories of my youth.

I step off the plane a stranger in my father's life.

On the truck ride back to his home, we hold arm's-length conversations about the weather, my grandmother's blood pressure, and the St. Louis Cardinals' woeful record last season.

When I walk through the door of his house, I will be a brother.

The excitement of my stepsister's bashful-eyed greeting bridges the gap of that first moment. My first morning, in this two-bedroom palace, we gather around homemade blueberry pancakes and blueprints of how we are going to remodel the basement.

This summer I am about to be nineteen. He is trying to be a better father than a long-distance phone call every few years. Since I was five, he has lived in Illinois, running away from a son for whom the state of Texas demanded child support. Within two years, he had a new wife and a new baby girl, far from the teenage mother whose dreams, at age twenty-four, he had shattered with a clenched fist. I was a child of guilt and inconvenience.

This year's birthday phone call was about how he was going to save me. Save me from drugs, the terror that comes from being a juvenile delinquent running the streets, righteous and unchecked, and my mother who is so twisted by mental disorder that she cannot see the escalation of my own. At the urging of my grandmother, frustrated and tired of my hiding in her house in Mesquite, I went. My father is seeking redemption, playing savior to a fatherless boy. I lap up the milk of his bullshit like a puppy.

Within a week, we transform the basement into four rooms divided by our handyman walls. Run electrical wires and stuff insulation between the two-by-four beams, nail up the Sheetrock, texture and paint the fresh, windowless bedroom confines. A bathroom is planned for the closet area. The living area will be for Melanie and me: a television, a couch surrounded by dollhouses, and Strawberry Shortcake cartoons.

As a boy, I betrayed my mother every time I said his name. I often took his side, and it was as if my words were his fist on her face. She paid the price for my overcompensating devotion to a false idol. I refused to hear the stories of his crossdressing sexcapades that bordered on rape. She could not get me to see the monster in the moonlight that would lead her to attempt suicide three times while I was still a child.

The second week we shop for a car and check out the junior college. I agree to work at the labor hall for three months, to save as much as I can and help pay for the car and insurance. This is the normal existence I have always craved: a family that shares meals at the table every night, and is deeply rooted in the community.

During the springs and summers of the late '80s, he has been clowning at Shriner parades, town picnics, and festivals all over Southern Illinois. His wig is a large yellow afro—

it starts the weekends in high fluff. The hick convoys rattle down the streets in miniature cars with obnoxious theme-music horns, rainbow-glitter-tasseled minibikes with lawn-mower engines, separated by the out-of-sync high school marching bands. The smiles of the children get lost in my father's large-shoe laughter as he bounces curb to curb in a zig-zag bumblebee dance, throwing candies to the outstretched hands on both sides. By nightfall, the clowns and the haggard blue-collar wives, Busch beer–waddling their Aqua Net hair-dos, find their way to the beer tents. The man-made fibers of that yellow wig feel like al dente pasta strands. My father, stranded behind the gooey sweat mud pile of white-face makeup smeared across his drunk-ass reality.

The first time I met the clown I was sixteen—we had just moved back from California, my life was already discombobulated. He appeared before me on a Saturday afternoon, unannounced and silent, in the middle of the birthday rush at the putt-putt golf course where I worked. Yellow wig, full face paint, ruffled orange collar, floppy shoes, staring at me across the Blue Bell ice cream freezer. I puzzled at this misplaced clown with a look that said, *What you want, dumbass?* as only a sixteen-year-old could. Thinking he was with one of the scheduled parties, I just stood there expecting a question or a name to pop out of his bright red mouth. Nothing but silence and our blue eye beams set on one another.

Running his face against every name I knew, I finally stumbled across, "Dad?"

Eleven years removed from Texas, he could not return to my life as himself. The spectacle made him seem heroic to the other parents.

I got an uncomfortable handshake, a hug, and, "I've missed you, son. So what are your plans for the week?" This was his way of saying, *I am in town for a visit, cancel whatever you have going on.*

The ensuing itinerary included daily gatherings at my uncle's house and outings to Dallas/Ft. Worth's typical tourist destinations: Texas School Book Depository, Six Flags Over Texas, Blue Goose Cantina, and various lakes and water parks. The only thing there wasn't room for was some time alone with the son that he missed so much.

My Illinois days start at five a.m. Thanks to my dad's connections through the Masons, I am allowed to put my name on the daily work list at the town local. The hiring hall is dingy, with wood-paneled walls and card tables where dime-hand rummy is played over coffee and work assignments. Farm-equipment ball caps and alcohol-withdrawal chain-smoke exhales are the only decor. During the good weather of summer, families with three generations of workers cram the tables looking for the best game, always determined by the old-timers' conversations, the room vivid with bloodshot eyes. Blue-collar workers that stuff a year's pay into a six-to-seven-month season, before the impossible workdays of winter send them to the taverns.

Every day for a month, I sit and listen to the stories of pouring concrete at the Sam's Club two summers ago in 110-degree heat. How Big Bill's son fell off the back of the truck and into the wet mixture as they leveled it out. How the farmland was being eaten up by the yuppies overflowing from the city. They all nod in agreement, casual, without regret.

My stepmother's dad, Grandpa Lewis, had owned the biggest pig farm in the county. He called me *Dallas* instead of Jason. The farm had been in their family for over one hundred years but when he died, none of his three sons or two daughters wanted to or was able to run it. The land was sold away, converted into two hundred thousand–dollar homes that stuck out of the landscape like the Volvo station wagons that crisscrossed the two main roads of town. They ushered in designer strip malls, traffic jams, and fat paychecks for the withered laborers.

Manual labor in the North is nothing like it is in the South. Illegal immigrants fill Southern roadways and construction sites, without union contracts and workman's comp insurance, for six to eight dollars an hour. Needing to feed their families, they wait in parking lots or street corners, jumping into the back of work trucks to be underpaid. I am eighteen and getting $19.60 an hour. It is the hardest work I will ever do.

For eight hours on the sides of country highways I dig ditches with a splinter-handled shovel and then cover them with straw. By the time I arrive home at five thirty p.m., dusty with straw embedded in my sweat-riddled clothes, all I can do is grab a beer and collapse. I have always found the American dream in the sound of a beer bottle cap popping off the glass. Earning a reward is better than having it handed to you.

This town of the hard-working, soon-to-be-extinct middle class lives for weekend festivals and picnics. Simple traditions that keep memories alive are the heart of every small town in this region. I remember the summer vacation trips as a boy: the fun of the Fourth of July parade, the fireman's picnic, late-night fireworks, sno-cones, and the whirling octopus ride that caused me to vomit the fruity red syrup all over my shirt and shorts, but never impeded my desire to do it all again.

The night my father learns I am a man, he is dressed as a clown. Sitting at a picnic bench, the concrete under our feet is a sea of crushed plastic cups and soiled napkins. Discarded cigarette butts resemble peanut shells under the canvas tent of the makeshift basketball-court beer garden. It has been a great Memorial Day parade and carnival by the looks of all the drunken clowns, some of who take turns squeezing the large breasts of one of the wives, and I give them high-fives for their efforts. The proud arm of my father is draped across his intoxicated underage son. By the time we leave, we are too blitzed to communicate across the twenty years of frustrated relations.

My half-sister, stepmother, father, and I walk back to the house on the other side of the park. Melanie plucks at my skin with soft pinches and teases. I jab back with a twisted, half-hearted, mean smile. I enjoy the annoyance of having a sibling. We are getting to know one another through sarcastic, harmless flirtations.

As we arrive at the house, breeching the backyard gate with a game of chase, my sister takes a spill rounding the corner. My right hand clutches her left shoulder as she tumbles onto the broken pebble path etched through the lawn. To those behind us, it appears as if I pushed her and then walked away. Only our laughter, trumpeting the small farming community night, suggests our true motives.

Once in the backdoor, you have to climb four narrow, steep corridor steps to a landing that turns left and climbs three steps higher into the kitchen. Melanie rushes into the bathroom, blood flowing from skinned knees. This one moment will hold my deepest satisfaction for years. It is the one single moment of my youth when I feel normal and whole. I am a son. I am a brother. I am convenient.

The next moment brings me back to the reality of my situation. My father, in generic Velcro-lace tennis shoes and homemade clown suit, catches me on that landing. His forearm rams my throat, pinning me to the wall, while his right delivers bruises to my cheek. Through the buzzed euphoria of disbelief, I hear him clearly.

"Why don't you push *me*, you little shit?"

The next four or five beats of my heart are like hourlong remembrances, flashing in uncontrolled bites at my consciousness.

The gun through the mail slot of our apartment when I was four: "Let Daddy in, he's not going to hurt you or Mommy!" The night he almost killed her, my mother collapsed half-choked against a dumpster in the back of the Safeway grocery store where he worked. The countless nights I was shuttled from my bed to my grandparents' back bedroom. My stepmother's black eyes bubbled up under Hollywood sunglasses during summertime visits. The dark weight of my father's touch on my life.

His eyes break at the smile restored to my face. With a guttural moan and heave, I turn him. His body snaps to as I shove him into the drywall.

This moment of reclaiming is like a slow breath, I will always remember the force of my knuckles and the blood of my tears. That busted-lipped clown hunkers to the wall a broken man who created a broken child in a cycle that repeats in ignorant desperation.

I stand over him vacant, forced back to that place I found myself in the dark as a child. Paralyzed by the same fear that controlled the cowering twelve-year-old boy, hanging on a fence and pelted with rocks. As an awkward friendless teen, I would embrace these demons by dissecting frogs with firecrackers down at the creek bed. Full-circle resurrection at seventeen, a vulture who hunted older men in porn stores and public midnight sex parks, proclaiming his place in this sinister world, a diligent student of the human craving for lust and love.

I am no victim. I am not my father's son.

CAUGHT IN THE ACT OF GOING NOWHERE
1992

"I CAN'T HEAR YOU!" I scream at my grandfather as I turn the stereo down.

My grandfather, J.W., stands in the doorway to his bedroom wearing a look of disgust. I did not expect him home this early. He did not expect me to be in his room, on his stereo, filling the neighborhood with John Coltrane. In fact, he probably did not expect his twenty-two-year-old grandson to be living in his house, hiding from the world, jobless, and stoned. The noonday sun sneaks through the cracks of the blinds, the horizontal beams fall across his reddening face. He looks like a pissed-off barbershop pole twirling in the August sun. We just stare at each other.

I wonder if he can smell the weed.

Even if he does, he will not say anything about it. We are a family adept at close-quarter avoidance. I live in his house, but we have not spoken in months. When I was little, he used to spend time with me. We went to Friday-night hockey games, and on Saturdays we got our "ears lowered"—as he put it—at the barbershop. I think the silence makes it easier for him. He never says the word "disappointed" to me.

"What are you doing?" he yells over the silence. "I can hear that noise down the street!"

"Poems," I say. "Just reading what I wrote this morning."

This is a typical day for me: I get up, I get high, and I

write poems on the floor of my bedroom down the hall. In the afternoons, I get high again and read what I have written out loud over the flow of the jazz. Some days I scream out Paz, Baraka, or Ginsburg. Every day involves the reading of poems over the max-volume of his stereo.

In the evenings, right after J.W. gets home, my friend Cornbread picks me up and takes me to his parents' house. We sit in his car five nights a week, smoking weed and bullshitting. Cornbread likes to listen to my poems. He also likes to show off his guns when the sun goes down. He has a TEC-9 and a .44 caliber revolver. Around midnight he takes me home. This is a great way to avoid my family; get up after they leave, leave when they get home, come home when they are asleep. I am going nowhere. My grandfather knows this. This is his first opportunity to tell me.

"Is this what you do all day?" he asks. "Waste your time?"

He also knows about artistic desire, more precisely the suppressing of his own passion, photography. When I was younger, he always had a camera around. He took photography courses at the community college. He created posterboard collages of his work. He showed them to no one. My favorite photo is a simple black-and-white image of his shadow stretching across the front lawn. The thick-shaded silence of his form, gigantic against the noisy brightness of the grass; the picture says everything there is to say about this quiet man. The photos gather dust in his closet under the darkroom equipment and a stack of *Playboy* magazines. I've looked at the magazines and the photographs often, over the years. Photography did not pay the bills or feed his children. A drawer of the refrigerator is still full of unused rolls of film.

"How is dreaming wasting my time?" I reply.

I have been dreaming of poetry in this house since I was seven. I wrote my first poem in this bedroom in second grade. In the summers, I stood in the dark stairwell listening for the muffled rhythms of the air conditioners, behind the closed doors of the upstairs bedrooms. Alone in the darkness, words flew off the top of my head out into the heat of the stairwell. My voice in harmony with the echoes that bounced back from the high ceiling; I kept time with the clatter of the air conditioners as I found the rhythm of my poems. I did not yet understand the power of the living poem and the way it connects with the muscles of my body. I just knew when I let the poem be spontaneous, I felt alive.

Poetry is my calling. No one seems interested.

"You're not dreaming," he adds. "You're pretending."

I just stare at him, embarrassed, not knowing what I should say.

How would you know?

I do not understand the sacrifices he made to raise my mom and her siblings. I have no responsibilities, no wife and kids counting on me. In the 1950s, marrying an older woman with a child born out of wedlock was neither common nor proper. My grandfather is both. J.W. was thirty-seven when I was born. I am my grandparents' fifth child.

"You're not a kid anymore, no matter how hard you try!" he says. "Or how often your mom and grandma try to baby you."

"I know." Truth is, I do not. I have no clue how to become a poet. More importantly, how I would make money if I did.

"Keep pretending and see how much time you have left for dreaming."

"Huh?"

"What you're doing here is pointless pretending!" he snaps. "Out there in the real world—that is where you dream! It's the only place dreams happen. Ain't nobody going to knock on our door and offer to make you a success."

I am really listening to what he says. There is a conviction behind his voice I have never heard. He has spoken more words to me in the last few minutes than in the last year. I feel the urgency in his eyes.

"One day there will be other things to think about. Dream now, while they still belong to you," he goes on. "If this is what you want to be, go do it. But do something! And leave my stereo alone!"

"Yes sir," I say. "I'm sorry for . . ."

He is already going down the stairs, leaving me with the echoes of his rant.

"Stop letting those two women save you! Spinning wheels go nowhere."

He is right.

The room seems vast and empty. I need to move out of here.

My life has been on hold long enough.

Cowboys Kill Indians so that G-d Could Survive
(after K. Coval)

White kid eats corn bread fried in a pan, greens stewed with oil and pork, black-eyed peas, tortillas, and grits—does not know that he is stealing—eats Swanson in tins, eats front-row prime-time, eats sausage in cans, eats helper, eats kraut,

                eats poverty, eats love, eats stories—learns of harmonious hate.

White kid knows jokes that his elders have said, knows Bunker, knows *Hee Haw*, knows locked car doors / through welfare check liqueur / stores, government housing / and descendants of slaves,

                knows Jefferson is trying to be like
                us. *Good Times* aint anywhere near.

White kid has white friends at white school, listens to white music, wears white clothes—

      he is flat-world mentality,
           speaks ___-wad ___-rod, this is the language
           of swings.

      He is told anything different is always a sin—white teachers, white chalk on blackboards, white walls, white fears, white news, white books, white faces behind the badges—he is good at spotting what does not belong.

      Has a black friend on the soccer team, comes to the white kid's party once—

told black friend his white friend jokes.

Has afro-girl *Penthouse* spread under his mattress—
has a Pam Greer breast fantasy on top of his mattress.

White kid uses racial slur when knocking on doors or fixing contraptions, watches *Roots*, finds it
                terrific/horrific. Thinks that is some shit far off in
the past.
         Andy Griffith Show whistles through the correlations.

White kid don't know, don't care, it will all work out tomorrow.
Thinks Christian, hates Jews—
                      They killed Jesus.
       Don't know how close it all is.   White kid knows stones
thrown from his tongue,
          —how connected it all is—   knows   pellets,
firecrackers, and crossbow   a friend made in wood shop.

White kid knows arrows
are weighted for things
words cannot break.
White kid rehearses stance before launches the shaft, rehearses
mockery consuming a straw
                —he carves himself from this salt.
          White kid feels alive, in the night, spun under high-
way halogens
             (lucid and penetrating, he is the pulse of
this nation).

White kid remembers how long he can breathe without holding his
breath,
how long he can breathe without holding his breath,
how long he can breathe without holding his breath,
how long he stands still without drowning.

WHY DID GRANDPA NEVER REALLY TALK TO ME
1993

"UNWED GIRLS DID NOT HAVE BABIES in 1952 Arkansas," my grandmother says as she stirs her coffee. "He was a beautiful man . . . I have made mistakes, Jase, been a fool sometimes."

I do not press her on what she means. I just smile as she watches my face, then turns to stare out the window into the balmy spark of the morning sun. I let the puzzle of family mythology piece together at her lips.

"Lindsey Porter Hall peddled his snake oil charms with a steel-blue eye." She exudes a flirtatious giggle, a sound I have never heard my grandmother make. As if she were a schoolgirl, a single moment of happiness blossoms on her face, the only smile to crack her frown in the four months since my grandfather's death. "We were going to be married the summer your mother was born . . . But my daddy did not want Lindsey to find us," my grandma adds, as her facial expression loses life. "We moved to Dallas overnight—almost as if we were sneaking out of Arkansas."

"Mom never told me about this," I say. A few moments ago, I did not know his name. Only that my mom had a real dad and I look just like him.

"Deb and I never really spoke about it either, she was just a baby. As far as she was concerned, J.W. was her father."

Her eyes fix on something in the backyard; beyond the

wood deck surrounding the porch, beyond the suffocation of all the suppressed memories of the past forty-one years. The guilt releases from her bones in heavy sighs. She married a man she loved and was with for over twenty-nine years. She has been in love with another man for longer.

"Jase, your grandfather loved you very much. He just had trouble showing it."

"I know he did." I do not believe the words I am speaking.

"The older you got, the more you looked like Lindsey. It bothered him that everyone recognized it." She paused. "Honey, you got the face of an Arkansas bigamist."

The serious undertone of her joke strangles my heart. Moisture wells up at the soft pink edges of my eyes. The harder I try to stuff the feelings escaping as salty tears, the more the face opens. I imagine the ghost of my grandfather stirring across the walls as his name is spoken. When I was a boy, he always had me on his knee or at the barbershop on Saturdays. I now know that as my boyish frame grew to resemble Lindsey's swagger, he became silent and withdrew himself from my life.

"Lindsey was a traveling salesman and had territory all over Arkansas," Grandma continues as she refills her cup. "I was barely twenty, worked at the bank in town." She livens her step as she crosses back to the table. "I had my own apartment," she says, sitting with a dancer's flare. "We were in love."

"So what happened?" I ask.

"Turned out he already had a family," she answers, as if it does not matter. Even though I can tell that it does.

"What did Papaw do?"

Her father, Ernest Morrison, held the family tight to his chest as if they were his connection to an eternal God.

"We moved. We lived happily ever after."

DESPITE THE UNEASY RESPONSE TO MY GENEROSITY, the couple smokes their pipe together like a pair of laughing hyenas feasting on a carcass. They load the bowl like there is no end in sight. I am amped by the situation. A captive audience makes me feel right at home. I decide to tell a story.

My story needs an introduction. I set the scene while loading a fresh bowl. I tell them about phone calls to my grandmother, fleeing across town to score dope, the lights of a cop car, and the Motel 6. They both look on in awe. I take a large hit, hold it, and begin the exhale. The smoke rises through my words.

"I check in to the Motel 6 at three this morning. Everything is chill for the first three hours. I go to my car to get a pack of smokes at six. A woman stands outside the side door as if she's waiting for somebody. I know she's a hooker, so I say, *Too early to be going to work,* as if she has not been working all night. I think nothing of it, head back upstairs. Now remember the sun isn't up yet. There's a knock at my door like five minutes later. I'm in my underwear lying on the bed. I ask who it is, a woman says, *Patty.* I open the door wearing only my underwear. Unfazed, she came right on in, decided I needed some company. Taken off guard, I look down both directions of the hallway, sure I'm about to be busted. Nothing. The audacity of this white woman, I think. I sit on the bed, she starts to undress, offers a trade for a hit. I am speechless. *A hit of what?* I ask. *A hit of the crack you've been smoking,* she says. *I will blow smoke on your cock,* she says. I try not to laugh. I've been up for a few days, and there was no sign of an erection on the horizon. She doesn't take no for an answer. Before she could get her panties down there was another loud knock on the door across the hall. We can hear a large deep voice asking if Patty is in here or not. Then the door next to mine. The man is loud and demonstrative. I think this is par for the course tonight. The man bangs on my door. I know for sure I'm being busted. She freaks out, gathers her clothes, and heads into the bathroom. She doesn't say a word. She knows something I don't. I hide my supplies under the blanket and sheets. Go to the door, with my jeans unzipped. This time it was a big, older black man, bald and pockmarked. He is steaming. Asks if his wife Patty is in here. I assure him she is not, that he is being too damn loud and needs to go away. He tells me to fuck off and give him his wife. I again say she isn't here. I'm nervous at this point; his loud behavior has lasted five minutes. Somebody's going to call the police. I tell him this and again that she's not here. He says he knows his wife was in here and she better not be smoking without him. He calmly turns and walks down the hallway back to their room. This was too much. I know a bust is going down today. Patty's hiding in the bathroom shower. I wait three or four minutes to retrieve her. She's still naked. The audacity of this bitch, I think. She puts on her clothes. I ask her to leave, she asks for twenty bucks for her time. I tell her she owes me forty for mine as I help her out the door. I know if I make a break for it, the cops will be waiting. I decide to be quiet, as if I am asleep . . . "Y'all want me to continue?" I ask, as I pause to light a cigarette.

"Hell yeah, this is a good story," he says.

"So there I am in the dark trying to be as quiet as possible, when the phone rings. I was taking a hit and the damn thing scares me so badly that my whole body jolts and the hot end of the pipe is shoved awkwardly into the corner of my eye. Now I'm in pain and paranoid. I answer the phone; Patty is demanding her twenty bucks. She says she's in the lobby and that I should bring it to her. I hang up, thinking this will go away. Wrong. She calls back three minutes later; I hang up. Then again. We do this dance for ten or twenty minutes. Every few times I tell her to leave me alone. The calls finally stop. Now I am hoping I do not go to jail. Ten minutes after the calls stop, the phone rings. The guy this time. Very angry, he demands that I pay her the twenty in either cash or dope. He says they know I have dope; they'll call the cops if I don't give them what they want. I hang up. These people are crazy. A couple minutes later I can hear him stomp up and down the hallway outside my room. He talks under his breath but I know he wants me to hear him. After a few moments, he returns to his room. The phone rings again. This time it's Patty. *You better pay me,* she says. I decide that I have to get out of here. I should have stayed, waited for my grandmother.

"I hurl down the stairs three at a time, sprint out the door to my car. I get to my car, notice the black man hanging out of his second-floor window. He screams about kicking my ass. I flip him off. Then I shout, *Fuck you!* as I climb into my car. I catch a glimpse of his figure when he leaps out of the window. Lands ten feet from my car. Pounds on the hood of my car, each fist landing in the same spot, making large dents. I tell him I have a gun; he says, *Shoot me, motherfucker.* I say, *I will shoot you, motherfucker.* We both hear a siren; an ambulance drives past the hotel. We look around. I am definitely going to jail. After three minutes of us screaming crackhead nonsense at each other, I suggest one of the onlookers is going to call the cops. He settles down, climbs in the car, and we talk. Long story short, he is mad his wife is smoking crack without him. Not that she sucks dick for the stuff."

"Dude sounds crazy," the panhandler guy says.

"Been a weird fucking day," I respond.

We all agree on this fact. They load a bowl. I load a bowl. I offer them the shower if they want. They both decline. Somehow, I think they expect me to make a play for the girl. I just want company.

"My turn," he says. "I got locked up a couple of weeks ago for about five days. She was alone." This story begins in a wrong direction. Young girls with drug addictions do not last long on Buckner. "She had a bad experience with a dealer who tried to turn her out."

"Oh shit, that's horrible," I say.

"Ain't the half of it. She goes over to score, but she doesn't have any money." He looks at her, says, "What did you think was going to happen?"

She says nothing, keeps looking down. Her body pulls tighter into itself. She does not like this story.

"They pass her thug to thug, all night long. All the crack cocaine she wants for as many black dicks as she can suck and fuck." His stare deadens. Mesquite, Texas boils just under his skin, supported by the look of betrayal in his gouged-out eyes. "How long were you there?" he asks her.

She does not respond. I get the feeling his question is rhetorical. The room fills with rage. He reminds me of my father, Mesquite, Texas, and me.

"All night long. Didn't leave until the sun came up. How many dicks can you suck in a few hours?"

She never makes eye contact with him, her frame as stiff as iron. I can feel the tears that build up behind her eyes. I feel like her whole being is about to rust.

"I'm still pissed at you for fucking all those niggers," he says.

My fists clench. The word *nigger* reminds me that I have grown to hate intolerance. Especially spoken by halfwits who blame the woman they supposedly love for being the cause of their own rape. I bite my tongue. You just do not do certain things in this world. Some of us are slow to learn.

The crack flows freely. The three of us miss the tragic truths of each tale. I let go of my tongue: "You shouldn't use words like that."

"Like what?"

"*Nigger*," I said.

A look of confusion falls over him, he does not understand my objection. I want him to understand this so I speak slow and clear. "What kind of home do you provide her?"

He starts to answer.

"Don't answer, just listen," I interrupt. "You hustle your life away five dollars at a time for what lays inside that so-called nigger's pocket. You rob, cheat, steal, and beg whatever it takes to get by for that day. You don't do it alone. You brought her into this mess. This young girl whose life is ruined because of your love and choices. Sounds to me like you're the biggest nigger in this story."

He does not seem to know what to say.

"We choose this," I say. "The choices I make to serve my addiction are no worse than the choices she makes. Who are you to blame others for our weaknesses? Don't want her to suck dick? Get her off these streets. But you want the drug more, so she stays."

The room is still, quieter than it has been all night. I feel a fight coming. I light a square waiting for his response, verbal or otherwise.

"You're right," she eventually says.

A smile sprouts on my face. She heard me. He turns his gaze to her. He is reluctant to speak. He stands over the bed, over the girl, over the mound of free rocks. He loads a bowl, draws in an enormous hit.

"Do you have a razor?" he asks. "I want to take a shower and shave."

"Hell yeah," I say. "A shower will make you feel right."

I am thankful there is not going to be an altercation. I am too high to fight. I give him a new razor and a can of shaving gel from my kit.

He enters the bathroom, stunned by the stand his meek girlfriend has taken. She looks at me and smiles as if to say thank you. Then right back to staring down, a position her head finds itself most comfortable.

What fucked-up event from her past convinced her that this was love?

She and I sit in silence. Her body twitches to a steady beat. She tries to move closer to the bathroom door. Trust does not come easy to her. She takes the smallest hits while he bathes. Careful not to waste any of the precious treasure.

T REMORS
1994

THE TILE IS COLD BENEATH MY FEET. Stillness lingers over the house. "Stop it. Stop it!" I scream. "Stop doing that!"

"What are you talking about?" Holly says. "I'm right here, baby."

"You know what you're doing to me, you fucking bitch!" I shout. "I can see you lying there doing that."

Her soft green eyes search my face for signs of coherence. Tears and snot run down my cheeks. She drapes her robe over my back, wrapping the pink terry cloth around my shoulders. Her nude body pimples in the frigid room; the closer she presses against my back, the more I shake. My knuckles whiten against the oven door handle. This happens too frequently.

We've been together for four months. Twenty-four years old, this is my first real relationship. It's normal at first, casual but committed. Every night is sexually adventurous. Her inhibitions never get in the way of what she needs in the bedroom. We share evenings of laughter, drunk and high. We experiment all over the house.

In the bedroom, when all is quiet, the ugliness of my childhood rears its broken head. She ignores this to the best of her ability. We spend our weekends at dinner parties with other couples; a large circle of friends who do not know the secret we are starting to share. This is my most intimate relationship. We laugh all the time, except in the middle of the night. Sharing a bed with a stranger is forcing me to confront my past. These episodes started two months ago. I have bad dreams. She tells me it is as if I am someone else. The person she knows is gone, replaced by a monster. She does not feel safe when the confusion and shakes take over. When the memories start, I am lost.

"Come back to me, Jason," she coos, stroking my hair.

My eyes fixate on the red second hand as it moves around the stove's clock. Every moment taking me farther from where this all began. I do not remember leaving the warmth of the bed and the bedroom. My breath falls in unison with her hand along my back. I grasp for something that will pull me back into the present.

"Stop doing that! Please stop doing that. You're hurting me."

The words barely able to form through my lips, the syllables jump and crack like a three-year-old's whimpers.

"You have to stop, you're hurting me."

"I'm not doing anything. Jason, this has been happening for thirty minutes. What's going on with you?" There is a panic in her voice, but the calm never leaves her hands.

"You know what you're doing to me. It's disgusting."

"Jason, you're not making sense."

"Stop doing that," I whisper.

"Stop rubbing your back? I don't understand."

I do not have the courage to tell her. I do not know if what I think is real or not.

"You're touching yourself while I sleep," I say.

"Touching myself?" She half laughs at the absurdity of my statement.

"Jacking off and laughing at me. What you're doing to me is sick and dirty. Quit laughing at me!"

We've done this hiding-in-the-kitchen thing six times now, each worse than the last, always ending with my screams about some weird sexual perversion. I accuse her and call her names. She is open arms with a soft touch, almost as if she recognizes the place I go even though she has never been there. She is two years older than I am, ten years more mature. She sees my promise through my scars.

Our sex life is not vanilla. I watch her masturbate, frequently helping with a hand or a toy. Holly showed me a freedom in sex I had not known before. Our whole relationship builds off our powerful sexual attraction, equal roles in the bedroom, not based on power like most of my other sexual encounters.

"D-don't hurt me," I stutter.

This is the first time I have been able to talk with her about what drives these situations. I feel like I am asking for help and accusing her at the same time. I want to inflict pain on her because I think she inflicts it on me. I do not know what is real.

"Bitch, better not hurt me!"

My teeth clench to point of near breaking, my muscles strain with a voice of their own. The oven door shakes violently. I do not want to call her names. Do not want to feel this rage and delusion.

Make it all stop. Make it all stop.

"Baby, I'm trying to help you," she says. "I just want to understand."

The other six times I've laid silent on the kitchen floor, crying until sleep retakes me. In the mornings, we never discuss the events of the previous evening. I usually do not remember them very well anyway. However, she remembers it vividly. I apologize as if I were sleepwalking.

"Jason, I'm not doing anything. I was asleep," she says. "Something's going on with you again, baby."

How do I explain to this woman I am falling in love with?

"Baby, you need to talk to me. I'm right here, you're safe." She starts to hum a song under her breath. I hear the words but the title escapes me. The melody rolls around my tongue. The muscles of my face unclench, exhausted. My knees unlock. My mind focuses on my surroundings.

"I'm in the kitchen, everything is going to be fine." I do not believe these words, but I speak them aloud anyway. The sweat on my forehead and back is cold. My toes cramp, sourness oozes through my stomach.

"Good, come back to me. I'm right here. We need to get you some help."

"I don't need help!" I snap.

"You wake up shaking and violent. Half the time, you don't know where you are. Yelling and making accusations. Jason, it's not normal."

I am crazy as hell.

"I'm fine," I say. In the back of my mind, I know what is happening. Yet I don't have the strength to admit the truth. When I dream, the taste of my father touches my lips.

Most of my memories flicker like short movies, where dialogue takes a backseat to sensations and smells. I can't piece it together. They are stilled movements, whispers, heavy silences. Flashes project in and out of focus, jumbled and disconnected. I can't control my mind in the dark. I have glimpses of his hairy, hard cock trapped beneath panty hose, moist harsh breath along the rim of my ear, a large hand collapsing over my genitals, the building lust of a voice telling me everything is normal. The older I become, the more I see *normal* as a word that, when applied to my life, means *imaginary*. Only tremors of emotion from the deep let me know that these pieces of memory are real, living somewhere within my little-boy insides, my body's memory.

"I thought you liked it when I touch myself," she says. "It's totally normal."

"I know," I respond, finally making a connection with her eyes. "Just stop hiding it."

"I do it in front of you; I don't have to hide. Baby, what is going on?"

"I'm all right," I say. "Just give me a minute."

"Jason, the closer we become the more this stuff happens."

"Everything's going to be fine."

"I got a number for counseling. You need to discuss this with someone."

"I'm fine."

"Jason, baby, you're not fine. You need help. Let me help you."

"I don't want to talk about this with anyone."

"Jason, if you don't get help, I can't be with you."

"Why do I feel like you're doing this to me?"

"I don't know, but someone has done something to you."

I already know who the dark shadow face is. My life is in shambles from the wreckage of his love.

"You can do this, you need help."

I look into Holly's face and find only compassion.

She doesn't want to hurt me.

I don't want to hurt her.

I don't know it yet, but in this moment her kindness has changed my life.

B LANK SPOTS
1994

FRAGMENTS—this is the way I recall my youth until I am twenty-four years old. A phone call with my father is the final breath of this life of lies.

"I remember the things you did to my mom."

He remembers too. No one forgets one-sided fistfights or the rage that will cause you to choke a nineteen-year-old girl. But it was not just the four years of confusion, which occurred when Daddy made Mommy a punching bag. It was my stepmother's black eyes during my summertime visits that occurred once every two or three years, from ages seven to twelve. There were midnight trips to his mother's trailer that were the only semblance of me having my dad, back when I went to visit.

"I never hurt you or your sister."

The truth of bathroom memory runs over me in a flood of shame and guilt. My fist tightens on the phone and the dangling noose I form with its cord in my free hand. I was five. My cousin was three and we played as usual in my grandmother's house. Shortly after dinner, we roamed freely, as the adults were happy to have us out of their hair while they watched *The Lawrence Welk Show* and *Hee Haw*. As the oldest grandson, I bossed Neil around, commanding how and where we played. For some reason I led him into the bathroom and locked the door behind us.

With an "Okay, Dad," I, without warning, end our phone call.

A feeling of enormity wraps around my lungs and sits me in silence and tears for an hour. An amazing sense of release comes over me and pieces that had been illusions in my nightmares for most of my life begin to fit together. This is a moment when I start to trust the voice inside myself and make myself whole.

The rest of that evening I replay the scene of what Neil and I discovered in that bathroom. We saw confusion and pain on the faces of the adults as we were hurried down the stairs to the safety of Christian morality and bleached-blond beehive country hairdos. I tried to make myself invisible by tucking my chin down into my chest, hiding my eyes under my thick white-blond hair. The adults surrounded us in the living room, standing above us as large as trees. I felt small. They were going to have answers.

My Aunt Barbra took Neil by the hands and asked what we were doing. My body clenched tight, I knew what we were doing was wrong. I broke the secret, our secret. This was the point that had caused so much frustration for me over the years, the shame of being dirty and bad. I had coerced my cousin, at five, to put his mouth on my penis; showing him how to use his tongue and lick it like ice cream.

I remember small details all the way through the struggling of the adults as they asked over and over how I had learned this thing. I remember my mother and grandmother squatting, holding me by the arms, looking into my eyes with the love only they showed me. I can see myself shaking my head, *No, no.*

Until this point in my life, at twenty-four, this is where my memory has stopped. The fierce head-shaking denial of a loving son. As the fog lifts, I remember the eye contact with my father that made me the keeper of secrets, the seeker of his approval; the good little boy who would never find love. His deep-brown eyes, there at the back of the living room. As if by telepathy, he carried the words silently behind the backs of my bewildered family members. I buried his secret for twenty years.

He was unsure what direction his son would take, silence or the shattering of monster-lust secrets; this could be his undoing. The secret the little boy kept fell from my adult lips. I saw him there, urging my silence. He was the teacher of a language I wish I did not comprehend.

I now travel freely the distance of the memory that haunted me with blank spaces and distorted fragments of time. The escape of my silence and my trembling knees; the urine that began to run down my leg that made the maternal figures before me distrust their questions. "Boys are just curious; it's okay to be curious," they sang with agreement and hugs, my grandmother taking a kitchen towel to the puddle on the brown tile floor.

"Sounds kind of wrong to me," my father responded nervously.

The echo of those words became the undercurrent of most of my life. On the way home, he questioned my mother as to why I was so fruity and what kind of sexuality his son was going to have. He gifted me camouflage, the hiding of fangs under a smile, the silence of a shut door down the hall from sleeping souls. He used the magician's touch of conjuring a shimmering fabric of lies to hold sickness together. The events of the evening were written off as normal by the time I was carried in from the car and placed in my own bed.

B ROTHER
1996

THIS IS THE DARKEST BAR, which is why they call it the Dark Room. I don't mind not being able to see very far. This means other people cannot see me either. I am nervous, feeling out of place. The glow of the red-glass candleholders illuminates the tables, from certain angles they appear to float in the air. From other angles, the candles appear to be the center of a wagon wheel. A crowd of twenty roll around the small tables at the front of the stage; twenty more hover at the back of the room, where the bar sits with a few large booths. The Dark Room is a rectangle with high ceilings. Though the space is not packed, it feels crowded. I am the only person sitting alone.

I am between homes. I live on a couch. Truthfully, I alternate beds at the apartment of two girls I know. I work at the world's largest porn store. I am twenty-six and the last years of my life have been chaos. Holly and I split up shortly after I started seeing a counselor. The therapy lasted a year after I moved out of her house. My sessions became performances of revealing poems about myself to the poor man. I became bored with the narratives and the single-member audience. I made him uncomfortable. I married a woman and divorced her within nine months. The night she hit me in the head with a frying pan, I decided to become a true poet. The only relationship I believed I needed was with poetry. I thought this exactly as I signed the papers. The divorce was finalized by early spring. It is now mid-September.

My life is not progressing. I promised myself to find friends who are poets. I realize a community of other artists will strengthen my resolve. Tonight, in this dark room, I am determined to live my dreams.

"Next up, we're going to have back-to-back poets named Jason," the redheaded host of the evening announces. Her name is Jenna Weatherly. I met her when I signed up to read a poem. She made me feel right at home, even though I have never been here before. Her bubbly personality off the stage is represented in the powerful, political, yet funny and almost cabaret poems she has presented so far. I think she is outstanding and beautiful. The crowd loves her.

"A first-time reader!" she says. I feel my stomach tighten and curdle. I think I am going to be sick. All of the sudden, I do not want to read my poem. But there is no backing out.

"Sporting his overalls," she says, "what are you, a farmer?"

The crowd laughs. My stomach sinks, my mind relaxes. I am wearing white corduroy shorts, a black T-shirt, and black canvas high-top tennis shoes. Not overalls.

"Y'all make a lot of noise for Jason Edwards."

Glad my name was not called.

I am nervous as hell. The crowd claps and cheers as the other Jason approaches the stage. One large man, in a booth off to the back, is excessively loud. He has a thick brown goatee and mustache, facial piercings, and glasses. He weighs easily three hundred pounds, looks like a biker. He applauds like a drag queen.

The poet, who seems motivated by the applause, wears overalls with one strap undone. His Doc Martens sport flames running down the length of the shoe, as if his feet are some kind of street-rod from the 1950s. His hair is a buzz-do and his face sparkles from glitter stuck to his facial stubble. There is something manly yet effeminate about this guy. He seems artistic as he nervously maintains a cool demeanor.

He pauses at the microphone. His paper shakes in his hand, the crowd hushes. We hear his exhale as he begins speaking: "I love you, Thom."

The large man at the back responds in kind.

That must be his boyfriend.

Jason E. begins his poem. The words are marvelous. He is exploring his own life. He casts a nonjudgmental light, which exposes his secrets and fears, on his own identity as a man. The poem speaks of his struggle to find love through sex, alcohol, and drugs.

We have a lot in common.

The words alone are not the most enthralling aspect of what he does on the stage. Power and passion project from the man. I feel like someone strung a fishhook through my gut, the taut line pulling me forward in my seat. Whatever tugs at me demands that I listen. The poem controls the room with a sense of identity, it navigates beautiful images surrounded by jagged truths. It springs naturally from his body. All of these things hold me in awe. He seems to represent exactly what I am looking for in poetry: a definition of self through the words. He is not just reading what he wrote. He is living the poem from deep within his body.

I have to meet this man. I have to know this man.

He finishes. The crowd applauds. A soft look of gratitude comes across Jason E.'s face as he leaves the stage. I cry a little, secretly, as a man does in the movie theaters, silently with a couple of teardrops stuck to the corners of the eyes. I am moved by his words, his experience through the poem, by the poem. I try to brush the tears away between claps without being noticed. I don't care that I have to read my poem next. My own work is the far from my mind. His poem is one of the most beautiful things I have ever heard. I know now that I came tonight not to speak, but to hear another first-time poet named Jason.

"That was Jason Edwards; give it up for him!" Jenna says to the crowd. While they cheer again, she takes a swig of her beer.

"All right, I don't know this next guy either. He's wearing some rocking Chuck Taylors. I don't know if his poems are any good, but his shoes are kicking ass. Give it up for Jason Carney."

The crowd respectfully applauds. As I approach the microphone, my yellow folded paper in my left hand, my legs shake. I notice Jason E. sitting with the large man; both focus their attention on the stage. The crowd hushes. I unfold the yellow paper. I hold the poem several inches above the black music stand to the right of the microphone. The paper vibrates from my terror of being on stage. I cannot stop the shaking.

I take a deep breath and the words just start to come out of me. Two lines into the poem, the nerves are gone. I feel alive!

My poem is about my father. The piece deals with issues of sexual frustrations and porn shops. It's about my search for self-knowledge and how it took me to some of the unhealthiest of places. The poem explores how lust can be an addiction, how sickness will repeat if not put in check. It's about the power a person has to perpetuate his sickness and force it onto others.

". . . *the past before the present, the addiction before the consent,*" I say, finishing my poem.

My performance lacked the power of the other Jason's piece. His poem was more skillfully presented. The crowd still supports me with applause. My senses are alive. The Dark Room smells like warm sunlight. I make my way off the stage and toward the bar. My torso covered in sweat. I don't make eye contact with anyone as I pass. Three minutes of standing still felt like running a marathon.

I need a beer and a shot.

"Shit, two good first-timers named Jason! Y'all clap loud for Carney the Carnivore!" Jenna makes a couple of more witty comments, hyping up the room for the next poet. "Y'all ready for a veteran? Give it up for the beautiful and talented Opalina." The crowd goes nuts as a house favorite comes to the stage.

I stand at the back clapping for the young woman, waiting to order a drink from the bar. The bartender is a pretty girl with shoulder-length curly black hair. The bright tattoos on her forearms stand out against her black uniform. She smiles.

"Can I get a Bud, please?" I ask.

"Make that two," another voice says.

I look over to find the other Jason standing next to me.

"I loved your poem," he says.

"Me too," I respond. "I mean, I loved your poem too."

"You ever been here before?"

"No."

"Us either," he says.

The bartender places the two beers down.

"And a vodka cranberry," the large man standing behind us adds.

"This is my boyfriend, Thom. I'm Jason."

"Nice to meet you," I say, extending my arm to shake both of their hands. "I'm Jason too."

The bartender sits the cocktail down next to the beer.

"We got this," Thom says, putting his hand over my wallet as I start to take out the cash. "On our tab." Jason E. hands me one of the beers.

"Thank you," I respond to both of them. "I will get the next one."

"Yes, you will," Thom says with a smile. Cocktail in hand, he heads back to their seats.

"Why don't you come join us?" Jason E. suggests. "I bet we have a lot to talk about."

"I bet so too."

M Y FAIR LADY
1996

"THANK YOU, COME AGAIN," I say, and hand the customer the black bag.

The store is busy for a Friday night. Hotrod had to stay on the register for forty-five minutes after I arrived. He is just now getting ready to leave at one in the morning. The grave-yard shift is long. Any time he hangs around after I arrive for work means two things: going to be a busy night and Hotrod will cut me a few lines from his dope bag. Both keep me busy, the sun will come up fast. Tonight is no exception. I do not enjoy his speed as much as the coke in my pocket, but it is the holidays. Be festive, I always say.

"It is there for you, good night," Hotrod says, out of the rows of videos and DVDs shelved behind the counter.

"You sure you don't want any of this?" I ask.

"No, I'm good."

"Thank you, be safe," I say.

The door to the office and counter area closes as he heads to his truck. Manuel and I help customers, while talking freely to each other, not concerned with customer service. We are nice to the customers, but it is a porn store after all and we are not here to build personal relationships. Jack off, suck a dick, let some stranger fuck your wife in the back, whatever you got to do (the people that come in here do some weird shit)—I don't care. Just hurry up and get the fuck out of here.

When the store is quiet or has less than fifty people, I write, rehearse, and snort things.

"You or me?" Manuel asks when his line of customers trickles down.

"You first, you been here longer," I respond.

He steps down off the raised platform and disappears into the shelves of pornographic films twenty feet deep. There are many thousands of titles. Behind the huge wood racks of plastic-covered videos and DVDs is the locked door to the office. In the five months I have worked here, I have never gone inside. The back area is quite large, but the sales floor is enormous.

This is the world's largest adult video store. We have more movies than anybody. The building is an old boat dealership. In front of me, the stacks, shelves, and rows of the sales floor go on for at least two hundred feet. There is pornography everywhere.

The counter stands a few feet above it all. Customers reach up to pay for their items. This U-shaped observation platform is the control center of this sadomasochistic Disneyland. On one side of the counter is a hallway leading to the thirty-six large, private viewing rooms. On the other side of the counter, twenty feet away, is a room containing thirty-two coin-op booths that accept bills of any denomination. These arcade-style booths are the more crowded of the two private-viewing options. All of them have a television screen with touch-pad controls allowing customers to scan sixty-seven different channels of porn. The channels and the store cater to a wide variety of tastes. We have a large clientele base seeking anonymous rendezvous in those spaces. However, it's against the law when it is two men having an encounter. Texas is one of fourteen states to have sodomy laws. We do not look the other way, but we do not look for it either. As long as no one acts like a fool, we are cool.

"Damn, that is harsh," Manuel says under his breath as he steps back up to the counter.

"Due back by midnight tomorrow," I say to the customer, as I turn to walk into the shelves. My turn.

"Hold on," Manuel says. "This looks like fun."

I turn to glance at the main door.

A silence falls over that area of the store as all eyes fixate on two women who have just entered. The first is tall and round. She is easily six feet tall and over 250 pounds. Her blond hair is long and curly, a shade darker than the boa thrown loosely around her shoulders. Her boobs appear lop-sided. She resembles an enormous globe in fuck-me pumps. She is all bright-blue body-hugging silk and Adam's apple. This drag queen looks rough.

"Oh shit," Manuel says.

I crack a smile at the other one. She is small, no more than five seven. Barely 120 pounds. Her black dress is more elegant than the one her friend wears, shimmering as she walks, and her costume falls across her frame in a natural way. Her pale arms are seductive, covered to the elbow in black satin gloves. Even her stride is graceful. Her hair, on the other hand, is outlandish. Super curly, a light auburn brown—from ten feet away she looks just like Barbra Streisand. She even has the big nose.

"Ladies, how are y'all tonight?" I ask, looking at Streisand.

Manuel snickers. Barbra tugs at her friend's arm, as if to say, *Stop here.* They saunter over to the counter, innocent as can be. They look a little tipsy, really out of place.

Most of our customers, I've noticed, are married men, unable to satisfy their sexual urges in their Christian mar-riages. I make a fun game out of patiently watching men loi-tering around the store. Sometimes, you catch them taking the ring off their finger, right before they cross the threshold into lollipop land. There is an uncomfortable complexity to the dance of masculine eyes as they bumblebee waltz, looking for a partner, waiting for the right man to come along. Each one of them reminds me of a boy I knew. I have pity for them. Life takes too much energy when you are living a secret.

"Don't y'all look beautiful tonight," I say as the drag queens reach the counter.

"Thank you," Big Blue says.

Barbra just smiles. She doesn't take her eyes off me.

"What y'all out doing tonight?" Manuel asks.

"We're partying," Blue says. "Looking for men, baby."

"I don't think you'll have a problem finding one here," I say.

The store hasn't had two drag queens cruise the back booths in the five months I have been here. I am nervous for them. They will be popular. Popular is not always a good thing. Their intentions are obvious. I am unsure of how to proceed.

"You're cute," Streisand says.

"You've been drinking," I respond.

"A little. Is it safe back there?"

"Of course," Manuel says. "If you don't bother anyone, they won't bother you."

"Is there anybody back there?" Streisand asks.

"Of course there is, it's Friday night," I say.

There is one thing you can count on in this business. Between one and three in the morning, right before and right after the bars close, nearly every drunk, horny, and lonely dude in the city comes through that door. All ages. All races. The one common trait among them is the thing controlling them between their legs.

"My friend said this would be fun," she says. "I'm kind of nervous, never done this before."

"What, never been to a porn store?" Manuel asks.

"Never come in to hook up with guys." Streisand blushes.

"Please," Big Blue huffs.

"You got to watch what you say," I tell Streisand. "There's no sexual activity allowed here at Star Adult Video."

"Oh, sorry. I thought . . ."

"Listen, what I don't see, I can't do anything about," I say. "Y'all just be careful, I don't want anything bad to happen to you. You're both way too pretty for that."

"You're sweet, and cute," Barbra Streisand says. "Do you got a girlfriend?"

"Actually, my friend Jason and his husband Thom recently hooked me up with a girl named Lisa." I smile.

"Oh, you got gay friends. Are you bi?"

"No, straight. Lisa and I have been dating almost two weeks. But you sure are pretty, ma'am."

I smile again, realizing how flirtatious I am being. Since meeting Jason and Thom a few months ago, I have been exploring my relationship with the gay community—going to drag shows at the Rose Room. I met Merle the gay cowboy at the Round Up Rodeo, a gay honky-tonk. They even got me drunk one night and took me to watch some buff gay stripper at the Village. He kept flinging his pecker at my face; I held out a dollar as if my arm was a twenty-foot pole. The year of our Lord nineteen hundred and ninety-six is an adventurous year for me. I guess that is why I am going out of my way to be nice to these upstanding ladies.

"Tall, handsome, and straight, I love it," Big Blue says. "ME-OW."

We all laugh.

"That is too bad," Ms. Streisand pouts. She raises her hand to her mouth, makes a blowjob motion with her arm. "Cause I would bop you off back there, if you would let me."

"Word," I respond without thinking.

Manuel chokes on his coffee. I stand there, stunned, big smile on my face.

Barbra Streisand wants to suck my cock.

This is better than the biker blonde last month, who wanted me to fuck her while her husband jacked off. My face reddens. "That's flattering," I say.

"You think about it," she responds, walking in the direction of the booths. "Just know I'll bop it good."

Damn that speed burns, I think as I step back up to my stool.

The store is busy with wanderers but the counter is empty. Manuel loads a movie a customer just returned into the VCR we have at the counter, checking to make sure it works.

The two drag queens disappeared into the back almost an hour ago. We have not seen them since. We notice several men come out of the back with unusual smiles on their faces. One even went back to the arcade after retrieving his friend. We believe the drag queens are getting popular.

"You think they're all right?" Manuel asks, staring into the monitor. "The little one seemed to like you, go check on her."

"Fuck you." I grin. "They'll be fine without me."

As I say this, the porter comes out of the coin-op booths and waves me over. He is the person who cleans the booths, restocks the shelves, and straightens the sales floor. He has the crappiest job in the place, and gets three dollars less an hour for his troubles. I am paid more because I can go to jail for selling pornography to undercover vice cops. Not to anyone else, only vice cops who are on the clock. A regular person off the street can buy porn from me and that is a legal transaction. Even an off-duty vice cop can purchase porn from us with no repercussions. We never know who the cops are, all the sales clerks get warrants. Sometimes they come into the store and take us down to the county lockup. The charge is obscenity. In Dallas County that charge carries a $1,000 fine and a possible 365 days in jail. The clerks turn themselves in to authorities when a charge shows up as a warrant. Jail hours are overtime. While locked in the county jail, I am paid time and a half. The store retains a lawyer who bails me out. I've amassed seventeen counts. I prefer sitting in jail three or four times a month, for eight to twelve hours each time, to cleaning up cum, piss, and other bodily fluids from the booths.

"Jason, come check this out," the porter says.

"Go ahead. I'll leave when you get back," Manuel says.

I make my way out the side door, around the counter, and over to the porter. He is smiling ear to ear.

"This is some funny shit," he says.

"All right." I walk with him through the threshold to the booths.

The back area is dark with a funky blue glow from the neon lights lining the ceiling. Small white circular lights mark the walkway on the floor between every door. The doors are black, in painted red frames. The room itself is a large square with a row of booths along both sidewalls. At the back, there is a small hallway; booths line both sides. Men mingle in this space, twirling like hawks over one spot on the floor. Tonight, seven men of various ages, race, and body types stand in two lines. One line contains three, the other line four. I've never seen lines like this before.

"What are they doing?" I ask.

"Just wait," the porter says as he exits back to the sales floor.

I stand there a few minutes, leaning back against one of the doors, smoking slowly on my cigarette. Usually when we are back here, the men scatter. These seven do not move. They don't even notice me. Soon, the door next to the line of four opens. A heavyset older man walks out adjusting his belt with one hand, combing his greasy silver hair with the other. He looks like somebody's grandpa. When he crosses out of the threshold, I see her.

On a folding chair, her back to the monitor, legs apart, and black dress hiked up to her thighs sits Barbra Streisand. She is smearing something across her chin with her glove. Her elegance has turned primal.

"Next," she says.

She stares at me. Her smile beckons as the next man enters. A look of complete satisfaction on her face, she disappears behind the guy's jeans as the door closes.

I smile, think, *Celebrate you, girl.*

The man that just finished passes me with a strut. "That was my second go-round," he says. "That little fag, he does it good."

"Really?" I reply, as he pauses to look at me. "Tell your wife hello."

His eyes grow large, then he quickly looks down in shame.

"Thank you, come again," I say, walking back to the control booth.

THE PANHANDLER GUY RETURNS from the bathroom, twitching. The lines on his face breathe, free of the past week's grime. His clothes tell another story. I hand him a clean T-shirt. The light of his eyes is almost sane; the blue pupils match the threads of the cotton. He stands at the bed, loads a fresh hit, and makes a spectacle of rejuvenation.

"You should take a shower. It will make you feel better," he tells her.

She stands up, enters the bathroom, looking at me before closing the door.

"You're safe here, I promise," he says. Then he sits on the bed, studies the porn movie, and questions me with his eyebrows. I can tell that he wonders about my kindness. Things are never free in his world. He leans back against the headboard, forming a sentence in the inhale of a hit.

"You sure don't mind sharing," he says. "You rich?"

"No, just dumb. Wasting a dead woman's insurance." I explain the situation with my mother's unexpected death. Falling apart is the only thing I know how to do. I tell him about poetry, my mom's struggles, and blown cash. He rolls his eyes at me in disgust and he offers a sinister cackle. As if he finally realizes my flaws. To him, I have everything: a room, clean clothes, money, and crack.

"Mine died when I was thirteen. She had cancer. I felt hollow since," he says, eyes frozen on the end of a flame. "Nobody really cared after that."

"I wasn't ready for her death," I mumble. "I should've been there." The tears start to flow out of my eyes like the money I've been wasting.

"You're mad. Your mom dies alone, her life cut short. How do you think *she* feels?" he jabs back.

"This is the longest I have hung out with anyone in weeks," I say, looking to change the subject. "I just feel like company."

"I bet she does too." He exhales, I inhale; the room fills with our disease. He turns his attention back to the porn on the tube. I stare off into space, stuffing my emotions. The pan-handler turns up the volume. A girl's voice demands something large inside of her. I look at the screen and laugh.

The first thing I see is Ron Jeremy's fat body, the hairs on his chest matted with sweat. A young woman in her early twenties is on all fours before him.

"He's got to be in his sixties," I say. "Been making porn movies since the '70s."

"How you think that girl feels fucking his old ass? *Oh, it's so big and you're so hairy and old.*"

He starts both of us laughing at the grossness that is Ron Jeremy.

"I saw him suck himself off in a movie from the '70s," I reply between giggles.

I do not say that I rewound the scene fifteen times that night. My fourteen-year-old self looking in the mirror as I stretched my torso over my leg propped on the toilet, trying to figure out how I could do this. Whacking my face against the bathroom counter when my mom called, I gave myself a bloody nose.

Our laughter dies rather quickly, the staleness of the porn a background noise to our next hit. As I exhale with a fresh rush, I ask him what I have been wondering all along.

"Do you let her trick as part of your hustle?"

"No," he harshly replies.

His sickness has its limits.

His love for her—twisted and wrecked. I can understand begging your way through your addiction. I have less than he thinks. Everything I truly have is on the other side of town, living their lives without me.

"That is the only thing I will not allow her to do," he adds. "She hustles for money at the gas stations, steals from the Walmart. Nothing bad."

He has the same twist of mind my father has. Prey becomes predator. I study his body language, thankful that I never shared this sickness with my wife. "Good. That's the right answer," I say. "She ought to go home."

"Well, thanks for the advice," he cracks a new smile. "She doesn't have a home. Neither of us does."

We load another bowl, inhaling what dreams we have left.

WE LEARN TOGETHER
1975

"TELL THE STORY, ANN," MAMAW SAYS.

"Let me get settled," my aunt replies.

Ann takes her place at the table, the women and youngest gather around. Stories always come with dessert at our family gatherings. Thanksgiving means dessert is either pecan or pumpkin pie. Craig and I sample both. The smell of fresh coffee brews in my great-grandparents' humble home, thick and earthy—a perfect undercurrent to the smiles and laughter of us all being together. My extended family is large: Ernest and Bill have four children, ten grandchildren, and nineteen great-grandchildren. When we all get together, the house overflows with gregarious laughter. I often catch Papaw eyeing the crowd with pleasure; the richness in his heart something money cannot buy. Money is something they do not have, do not need. Stories are the currency of our family; most everyone fills the coffers during our family gatherings. Papaw sits at the card table with the rest of the men, within earshot of the conversation.

"A year ago July, Craig and I came to a stop at a traffic light," Ann begins. "He was only five then, still young enough to know when you speak and when you don't."

The room instantly falls to a hush. Storytellers receive the utmost respect in our family. All eyes settle on Ann, waiting to hear this tale that most everyone already knows. At five years old, I do not. Most of the family yarns and anecdotes are history lessons. I am eager to learn.

"Lord it was hot." She fans herself, adding a theatrical element to her tale. "Hot enough to fry an egg in the dark." Everyone giggles.

I love how Annie tells stories. Bright and vibrant, like her blue eyes. Annie is my second mom. I love her accordingly.

"It was late at night, by the way, nine or ten."

"That's what makes it scary," my cousin Viv says, moving her hand across my shoulders. "Got to learn to lock your doors in this town."

Viv, one of the grandchildren, is seventeen years old. Craig and I fawn over her and her sister Kate as if they are beauty queens. We steal as many kisses on the cheeks and hugs as they can muster during our holiday traditions, our faces a collage of pink and red lips by the start of the fourth quarter.

"So we're at this light, just dropped Jill off at Dana's house for the evening, and this car pulls up beside us." Ann pauses for a quick bite and large gulp of coffee.

"A convertible," Craig adds.

"That's right, honey, the car was a blue convertible," Ann says. "A really nice one, Daddy would've loved it."

Papaw, born a sharecropper in Arkansas, is now a mechanic in Dallas. He has an uncanny ability to fix things. One of his many manpowers, as I call them, is that his eyes can see right through things immediately, detecting the problem. He loves working on cars.

"So I am admiring the scenery, sweating wildly."

"You mean fixing your face in the rearview," Uncle Arley interrupts with a wink, grabbing a small sliver of pecan from the pie tin.

"Arley, hush up and go back to the card table." Mamaw slaps him lightly on the backside, more irritated that her son's blocking her view and using his hands than the interruption.

"Craig's in the backseat, staring with curiosity out the window," Ann continues. "All the windows are down of course, too hot not to be. Real quiet out that night, not very many cars, but the red light was taking forever." She eats a bite of pie; points her fork as she chews and speaks. "I was lost in the delay, the humidity, and the song running through my head. I just love Neil Diamond."

"Oh, I know. He's really talented," my mom says.

"We should go see him next time he comes through town, Deb," Annie digresses.

"Get back to the story." Mamaw does not care for Neil Diamond. "Everyone knows church hymns are better than that rock-and-roll hubbub."

"Mamaw, Neil Diamond isn't rock-and-roll," Viv corrects her.

"Child, better listen to your mamaw or go get you a switch," Mamaw snaps with a smile. "Now get on with the story, think you're telling about Moses with all the time you're taking."

A chuckle falls over the room. Mamaw's threats are often funny, but never to be taken lightly.

"So I'm off singing in my own little world, when all of the sudden Craig yells out at the top of his lungs," Ann pauses for effect, *"Hey, Mom, look at that car, it's a bunch of niggers!"*

"There *were* a bunch of niggers," Craig affirms.

"Stunned, I look over at the car idling next to us," Ann's voice grows higher with excitement. "Sure enough, staring right back at me was a car full of niggers. Sure enough, everybody heard Craig."

Cousins and uncles and sisters and mothers laugh and gasp in shock. The energy of the room swells, anticipating the comical outcome to the situation.

"I about peed my pants right there. I was so damn scared

they were going to get out of their car and get me. So while we are all staring at each other, I floor it."

"Oh Lord," my grandmother Freeda says.

"Our tires were peeling out," Craig interjects. "It was so cool!"

I think this is so cool too.

"Without even looking, I barrel through the intersection," Ann says. "Wouldn't you know it, but at that moment the only other car on the road is crossing my path."

Viv is laughing so hard with my Aunt Barbra that they both start to snort and cough.

"Lord was looking out for us, we shot right at that car and missed T-boning it by barely an inch. The driver's face all lit up with fear. I bet he peed himself too."

The room is laughing so loud, I swear that the ghosts of our dead ancestors bellow behind us. The levity being the fact she almost hit another white person because she was so terrified that the black people were going to get her. I am too young to understand that part. I am the only one pretending to laugh. I smile, staring around the room for a connection that I can understand.

"Those niggers put a fear in me," Ann says with a smile. "Craig almost got us killed."

Viv leans in to me, places her hand upon my knee. Her soft eyes focus on mine as if she is going to tell me the most important secret. "Jason, niggers are black people," she explains.

I just stare at her blankly. *I know that already.*

There Are One Hundred Punch Lines to the Following Question

Boyhood jokes made us laugh

to tears.   In the park, young prophets
of our parents hate. After the jokes, we pretended   to be
                         pro athlete black, taught

the difference between *boy* and men.   Tony Dorsett
                         was the one that I liked.

How many dead ni__er babies nailed to a tree?

S HOW TUNES AND HATE CRIMES
1997

"HELP ME!" JASON EDWARDS SCREAMS. "Help me!"

He explodes into the house, blood running down the side of his cheek, a red welt on the side of his forehead. One strap of his overalls is torn and undone, the buckle at the end twirls around his body. Jason E. runs in place, looking for safety. His feet covered in soot and water, carrying one Birkenstock sandal in his right hand. He is exhausted and near collapsing.

"Help me! Help me!" he cries hysterically.

I am at a loss. I look at the clock, about an hour until midnight.

I have to leave for work in thirty minutes.

I stand puzzled, wearing a white button-down shirt, a pair of jeans, and a red necktie that I am in the middle of tying. My mind tries to process where the hell he just came from. Earlier in the day, when Thom went to work, Jason and Michael Loris went drinking down the street. The plan was to take a taxi back to the house. As I am learning quickly, Jason and Michael didn't follow the plan.

Jason and his boyfriend Thom, along with Lisa and I, have been living together about a month. Lisa and I have been dating for two. She is on an overnighter, which is common for flight attendants. When the four of us are together, we party every evening. Michael is often involved; this house is always full of craziness, just not this kind. A few seconds pass before I can figure out what to say.

"What's going on?"

"They attacked me. I ran, help me!" he screams.

"Who attacked you, where?"

"A gang . . . down . . . at the corner," he struggles to say as he catches his breath.

"Where's Michael?"

Michael Loris is a small man. He can't weigh much more than a hundred pounds, barely five six. Flamboyant to say the least: he wears a full-length baby-skunk fur coat, smokes from a long black cigarette holder, and carries a large purse that looks like Chewbacca's ass hair. He is an actor by trade. His personality is larger than life, often presenting a Jekyll-and-Hyde switch. Sober, Michael is charming. Loris the drunk, however, is anything but congenial. One night he busted into our bedroom while Lisa and I were having sex. He yelled, "Slap her pussy! Slap her pussy!" When I am fucked up he amuses the shit out of me. Not everyone is going to be so patient with him.

"We got drunk," Jason E. explains, his breath slowing. "Decided to walk home, down Maple."

We live on Kings. This side street connects to Cedar Springs and Maple. These two main avenues are very different. Cedar Springs is the gay mecca of Dallas. Gay-owned businesses and bars line the street; side streets in both directions are gay-owned houses and apartment complexes. There is a party atmosphere to this neighborhood most nights; even with the Jesus freaks who hand out *Homosexuality Is a Sin* pamphlets to everyone passing by. One night, I heard a gay man refuse a pamphlet. "No thanks, I am going to be sucking dick in heaven." I love living here.

The gay and lesbian community of Dallas embraces itself when others do not. Even with all the protection that comes from identity and numbers within this neighborhood, the Oaklawn area of Dallas is not always safe. For every *Homosexuality Is a Sin* pamphlet there is a flyer informing the residents of recent violent attacks in the community. People have to be alert here, especially in the dark.

"We were skipping and singing show tunes . . ." he continues.

Maple Avenue is not the place for *The Sound of Music*. The barrio rages down the pavement. Cracked sidewalks allow weeds to grow through as a habitat for the vagrants who panhandle for change to cop some dope or beer. The roadway is potholed so deep that rainwater never dries out in the sun. Signs in English and Spanish hang in the windows of the stores. Gang graffiti litters the walls of the empty lots and closed-down shops. Some of the first-generation Americans struggle to adapt to the idea that these streets are the dreams white America is offering, not a safe haven for gay boys.

". . . then they attacked us." He is starting to get hysterical again. "They had sticks and golf clubs."

"Where's Michael?" I ask with more urgency. "Where is he?"

"I'm sorry, I left him! I just ran," he cries. "There were so many! He's at the store on the corner—I ran home."

Without thinking, I fly out the door, my red tie flopping with my strides. I fumble with my Corolla keys, jabbing at the door with the handle of my key chain. Finally getting it right, the worst scenarios run through my imagination. Gay men in this country have been stabbed, shot, hung on fences, beaten to death, and set on fire, killed with fervor for just being the person our Heavenly Father created. I have been guilty of hurting these men. This is the first time I am truly confronted with the terror my past actions caused other human beings. I picture Michael stabbed or shot, balled up on the side of the road.

Just don't let him be dead.

"You got to go help him!" Jason E. yells from the patio, just outside the back door.

I turn the ignition, throw the subcompact into gear, pull back out of the parking space. Before the vehicle stops rolling in reverse, I throw it into drive. The Corolla jolts.

I can do this. Come on, go, car.

I do not have any preconceived notions of kicking ass and taking names. I am not going to the convenience store to win or look cool. I just want to get Michael and survive. My family taught me that friends help their friends, especially when they are in danger. The little engine revs as the car climbs to the exit, sounding like a swarm of cicadas hidden in a tree. I have never participated in an act of atonement, or done something for the right reason when the act may cause me harm. The car zips toward the store. I feel like I am free-falling on a bicycle as I plunge toward the unknown.

Hang on, Michael. God, please protect us.

I am so fucking terrified.

THE BATHROOM DOOR OPENS; steam fills the silence between the panhandler guy and me. I smell the hideous nature of what has been washed down the drain. She exits. Her hair wrapped up in a towel, she looks ten pounds lighter. The comfort starts to return.

"Y'all want toothpaste?" I ask.

She nods her head yes. I walk over to my shaving kit, offer her the tube with an outstretched arm. She holds out her finger.

"How about you?" I ask the man.

"No thanks."

She starts brushing her teeth with her finger. No water, no sink, just the minty scald of the paste to her raw gums. She seems invigorated.

"You want some water?"

She nods her head again. I point to the bathroom. She rolls her eyes.

"Last hit," he says.

I break down what is left of my slab, tossing him a few rocks. She steps back into the room. Their renewal process over, they both sit down in their original positions. He loads his girlfriend a fresh bowl.

I need entertainment. I focus on the door. One of my favorite tweaker games is Freak Out on the Door. Simple to play: Take a hit, then waste your time constantly going to the peephole checking for anyone. Once you sit back down, stare at the handle for movement. I mean really *stare* at the handle as if everything in the world depends on it remaining motionless. After a while, convince yourself that it does move. Focus on the *Do Not Disturb* sign as if you are sure the placard is wiggling. Then get up. Do the peephole thing again. If you are not freaked when you start, you will be by the time you make the third cycle. Back and forth. You can do it for hours before you realize how fucked up you are. With more than two people, you may have a very interesting spectacle. A simple suggestion can create a centrifugal force spinning a doper into hell.

I start the game off: I get up, stand at the door for a couple of minutes, then walk away. Then one-step back to the peephole, as if I heard something. Reluctantly, I return to my chair. My gaze fixes on the handle, the chain. Silence fills the room again. In just a few slow minutes, I have their attention. The game is underway!

"You hear that?" I say. I stand, the blood rushing from my head. Wooziness stumbles me the first three steps. Regaining composure, I make my way half blind to the door. My shut eye presses against the peephole. They talk to themselves about what I hear, what I see.

"Y'all be quiet a minute." I sway, peeking through the glass-covered hole.

"What is it?" the guy asks.

I return to my seat, fixating on the handle. "Did you hear that?" I ask.

"I did," she says.

"Go check it out," I say.

She crosses the floor like a ninja, leaning against the door ever so slightly.

We have a winner.

I load a fresh hit and watch the spectacle unfold. For ten minutes she stands at the door. I sit smoking.

Does she see what she thinks she hears?

She returns when her boyfriend calls her over for a hit. Now she is in a constant panic, watching the handle. I say nothing else. One statement followed by a simple action causes her to spend the next thirty minutes going from bed to door, door to bed, her only salvation the thirty seconds every once in a while when her lips suckle on a metal tube.

The guy figures out what is going on, but he is powerless to stop the whirl of her paranoia. We both lose interest in her debacle. I begin to feel bad. Just as I am about to tell her to sit down, that I have been fucking with her, she darts to the bed.

"There's a black man at the door dressed in a uniform," she says.

Pangs of death fall over us.

I am not about to fuck around. Without a noise, I glide over to the door, listen for a knock, a faint breath out in the hallway, voices climbing the stairs. There is only silence.

Is she fucking with me?

She is prone. Arms nestle under her frame; she shrinks to the carpet.

Surely not.

Crackheads are great liars but horrible actors. If you can learn to tell the difference, you will never be cheated with fake dope.

"Are you sure?" I ask, confusion and panic rattling my brain.

"Yes, he bent down when he got to the door," she whispers.

The guy and I stand frozen, the bologna sandwiches of the county jail racing through our brains. He shuffles to the window and checks the edges of the curtains.

"I don't see any squad cars," he says.

The game turns on its side now, a sense of reality dosing our spinning heads.

This is going all wrong.

No one breathes. He and I glance at each other, then the door, then at her. No squad cars, no knocks at the door, no sound rushing through the hallway—only four minutes of silence.

We begin to breathe again, still unsure of what the fuck is going on. I approach the door, slowly caressing the peephole open this time. Nothing lingers in the hallway. I decide to open.

"What are you doing?" he asks as I undo the lock.

"Oh shit," she whispers.

There is nothing in the hallway and no one on the stairs. I peer down the hallway, then down at my feet. A piece of paper lies on carpet right at my feet. The receipt for my hotel bill. I begin to laugh.

I explain that the security guard left my bill. Their tight faces show relief. No bologna sandwiches today.

"Fuck," he says with a deep exhale.

As the girl stands, my cell phone goes off. We all jump. I sit back into the chair, load a fresh bowl, and check my phone.

C has texted me, wants a favor. Tells me to be there at two forty-five a.m., a package needs delivery. Something doesn't feel right about this. I debate not getting back with him.

He is not going to take no for an answer.

"Y'all, I've got something to do," I say. "Where can I drop you at?"

"At the Racetrack on Bunker," he quietly replies.

The location could not be more perfect. Four minutes to the apartments where C waits. They gather their stuff; disappointment flows over their frames. Her body seems to grapple with the exhaustion of having to go back to the street. For the first time, I really grasp how easy the past few hours of her life have been.

We exit the room. No one talks as we travel down the

stairs. I feel guilty. As I reach the landing, I turn to look back to the stairwell entrance.

"Y'all hold on one second," I say, "I forgot something."

I return to the room. As I insert the key, I check to make sure I am alone. Shut the door behind me. I climb to retrieve a hundred-dollar hunk from inside the smoke detector above the bed. I put the rock in my pocket, leaving the smoke detector hanging from the ceiling.

I will fix that when I return.

I thank them for waiting. The first three minutes of our drive is quiet. All of us speed in our own directions; a haze floats over the car. I cannot stand the silence.

"Where y'all going to stay tonight?"

"Hopefully we can scrounge up enough dough for a cheap room before dawn," he answers. I can tell he is waiting for me to offer them one of the beds back in my room.

My generosity is evaporating quickly. I head down the highway to East Dallas. I begin to think of my mother. The girl in the backseat is someone's daughter, even if her parents do not love her. Sacrificing her youth to the hands of this man who is not much different from my father, from myself. I make a spur-of-the-moment decision, the voice of my mother somewhere in my head. I exit one stop early, travel the service road entering the parking lot of the Mesquite Inn and Suites. The Racetrack is only a quarter of a mile away.

"What are we doing?" he asks.

"Wait here; I'll be right back," I say as I open the car door.

I walk inside, pay for two nights in the cheapest room they have.

This is the smartest thing I've done in days.

The clerk hands me my change. The whole act takes less than five minutes. I head back to the car smiling.

"I have a friend that stays here; let's check it out," I say.

We drive around to the side of the building, the parking

lot lit up and quiet. I imagine hookers, crackheads, and maybe an unsuspecting tourist hiding behind the three or four rooms whose lights peek through the holes in the curtains. I pull into the parking spot right in front of the door. The guy and I move quickly out of the vehicle, we do not speak, we both want a hit. I turn to look at the car as I stick the card into the slot. She climbs out, ten steps behind us. I wait for her to catch up and I hand her the key. "Y'all can stay for two days."

They do not say a word, their faces twisted by the absurdity of my actions, an unheard-of kindness. To me, out there in the darkness is a mother, unable to sleep, wondering what bad decisions her eighteen-year-old is making. We enter the room.

King-size bed, cable television, a shower, it's nothing special, but more than she has in her life right now. She jumps on the bed like the teenager she is. Arms spread out above her head, she makes snow angels on the comforter. Even lets out a little giggle.

I reach into my pack of smokes. The large slab is easy to grab. His eyes light up as he catches the rock in my hand.

"Let me borrow your pipe," I say.

He already has it out, anticipating more good fortune. I load a very large bowl, the crumbles flow over the edges like the head of a root beer float. I strike the lighter. Inhale deep. The sweet sensation envelops my head. I almost pass out from holding my breath too long. I throw the slab of crack on the nightstand. Walk out. I do not say a word. Neither do the couple.

In the car, my mind swirls with an uneasy feeling about going to C's.

I hate doing favors.

I hate this cycle of addiction. The nonsense will not end without a catastrophic event. No matter how many panhandlers I help, until I save myself, I am heading toward disaster.

She will sleep in a bed tonight. The first small victory to put a smile on my face in months. *For the next couple of days she will not have to beg to feed her boyfriend's habit.*

I feel that this is somehow going to be my last act of kindness. I start to cry. I sense disaster floating close around me. I am exhausted.

My car drives itself down the service road.

SMOKED-OUT TOOTH

I sand my teeth with metal emery boards,
catch dust of enamel and tin on my tongue.

The back of my mouth bleeds congestion and
stale euphoric memory of the high. It tastes

of gasoline and disease. Chrome pus
floods my gums when I laugh and clench.

My bones quake to stand still. I am faced
opposite of yesterday—the warm melted

smell of cannibalism licks my neck. I will
not turn to its truth. Relinquish trophies

that stab my cheeks. I will grind smooth
spit-shine stars from their blackness.

FAITH WITHOUT WORKS
2005

"THE CHOICE IS YOURS," I say. "I can only show you what I was taught, no grand revelations here, man. Only hard work."

"I know," he responds. "After hearing you tonight, I think my ideas may not be so right."

When I offered at the beginning of my show earlier tonight to talk to any of the six who committed the hate crime on campus, I didn't think I'd have any takers. This was not the first time I've had to address such issues at one of my shows. At the University of Virginia a few years back, we did a show shortly after the first African American girl to run for student president was beaten by white boys using racial slurs as she walked across campus. Last night, security cameras caught six young men spray-painting hateful slogans all over the campus of this small public university, located in upper Michigan, in protest of the drag show that the gay and lesbian student organization sponsors every spring. One of the more sedate scriptures that they painted on a wall: *Bring a shotgun to school and kill a fag.*

By the time the sun came up, the campus was covered in a sickness and ignorance colder than the April snowfall of a few days before, now littering the ground, embedded with dirt and grime. The only spot of cleanliness I noticed when I arrived on campus this afternoon was the public outpouring

of support for those harmed by the act. Even the state repre-
sentative for the district came by and got his photo-op: one
politician, three hundred students, and the university employees wearing black T-shirts with the slogan: *Gay, Fine by Me.*

This student, not admitting to being one of the six, and
I have been in my campus hotel room—a small room above
the school's kitchens used for administrative guests and visiting professors—for about two hours, bullshitting and telling
each other stories about our raucous youth, while I gather
and pack my belongings. I am tired. The chill of the night
outside settles across the room. The show tonight is my last
for the current school year. I did not expect this one to be so
eventful, not anticipating this chance to make a difference,
and I feel discombobulated in my approach, pausing several
times during the course of our conversation to pray silently
within my head for guidance.

At six in the morning, a cab is coming to take me to the
airport. I did not intend on being up this late. The enormity
of this moment has not reached him yet. I can see myself in
his twenty-one-year-old eyes. I pull a legal pad from my backpack and the ballpoint pen from my shirt pocket. He seems
intrigued, as if I am doing a magic trick, removing what we
do not like about ourselves to somewhere far away.

On the paper, I draw two lines, creating three columns
with the largest on the right. In the first column, at the top
of the row, I write the word *nigger*. It's a word that we as a
culture have created, used solely for destructive purposes, and
implemented over the years to differentiate and denigrate fellow citizens who we could not contain but tried to confine.
His eyes light up with an uncomfortable stare. Every white
person fears the discussion of this two-syllable word of hate
because it begins with guilt and ownership and accusations
that have always been true of this privileged white culture. I
learned a lot over the years, watching even the most liberal

white citizen hide true emotions in the guise of politically correct bullshit slogans, such as: *I got black friends* and *I never
owned any slaves,* or *I am Irish and we were treated just as
bad as the blacks.* Instead of addressing the problem, and col-
lectively moving on to a better definition of not what past we
are hiding from but rather who we have become out of those
errors and regrets. Even worse when done with sophistica-
tion and advanced rhetoric such as *black-on-black crime* and
black-on-white crime. I discovered white folks have a strong
dislike toward discussing *white-on-black crime,* even though
its origins allowed for freedoms and wealth to be created.

We sit in silence for a few moments.

"If you take inventory of your life, you'll have a better
understanding of who you are and the world around you. If
you don't define yourself and the world, then the world will
define you. And that's limiting to your identity and the possibility of achieving your dreams."

In the middle column, I write a few short sentences describing the first time I learned that word from my family. I
give him the brief outline of the tale as I write. He laughs at
the story, catching himself and trying to suppress his emotion.

"It's okay, laugh," I say. "It's a funny story. That's the
point. In this country we teach hate with laughter and love.
You didn't invent this anger and hate inside of you, you
weren't born with it either. Somebody taught it to you."

"I don't know, seems like this is the way I have always felt."

"That is what I thought," I say. "I'll prove it to you."

In the third column, I write the word *family.* Under that I
write words associated with what I felt hearing the story, and
how it affected me and my actions. When finished, I move
back to the first column. I write the word *gay-rod.* Next to it,
in the middle, I write down *boys on the playground.*

"I called a white boy *nigger* on the swings and he called
me a *gay-rod* and a *gay-wad.* I told him that I didn't know

what those words meant, so the kid's older brother explained them to me."

I write down my age: *five*. Then in the third column, I write down the word *friends,* under that the lessons I associated with *gay-rod*. The deeper I go in the third column, the more actions appear because of the knowledge of the first and second columns. The causes and effects become quite clear.

"I'm not responsible for column one and two," I say, "but column three, those actions are mine. I have to take responsibility for them. Do you see what I'm doing here?"

"Yeah, I get it. But how does this apply to me?"

I slide the pad over to him. "Think back. What was the first racial slur you remember hearing?"

"How's this going to help?"

"Every thought, action, fear you have had since you were little has been built off a foundation. We're looking for the cornerstones, so to speak."

He picks the pen up, thumps it on the pad as if it's a drumstick. His brown hair hangs down over his forehead, his face hidden from view.

"If we discover the what, when, how, who, and why of your beliefs, then we can see their virtue or their failure," I add. "Writing that shit down gets it out of our head, and onto something that we can control outside of our self—the page. We can rewrite the page, thus changing ourselves in the process."

"I've always looked at the world just the way it is." He shrugs. "Some things are just the way they are."

"Faith without works is dead."

"Huh?" he responds, as if this is the most complex thing he has ever heard.

"Once you start to do this, you will never look at the world the same way again. You're going to have to be around your family and friends, their attitudes and beliefs, their actions and speech."

"Yeah, that sounds hard," he says. "I don't think I could change my dad or my friends."

"It ain't about changing them, it's about being an example to them. Your actions are the example to them, as well as your speech. We are getting ahead of ourselves. Let's start with *you*."

"All right," he says.

"Just know, if you do this, if you start to change your views and redefine yourself, the world will test you. At some point, you'll have to take action and live what you've learned. That is the karma of personal growth. Faith without works is dead."

"I think it's my father," he says. "The first time I remember hearing the word *fag*, he and his friends were beating some gay guy up. They left him in a ditch."

"Did that teach you something, mold you somehow?"

He looks at me as if he is about to say something, pauses, then looks back down, the pen in his hand pressed against the yellow paper. Again, he looks into my face, this time he smiles. He stares at me, content, as if somewhere deep within the core of his being a light switch just flicked on. He begins to write.

VESSELS AND GONE
2007

I SAT ALONE, removed from the woman in the box with her seizures and migraines that withered her into nonexistence. Feelings of regret and remorse brought me to this pseudo-sacred room of cold goodbyes to an empty vessel. Without her spirit to occupy it, her human form makes a mannequin of her flesh. The body only resembles my mother.

She never liked funerals because everyone sobbed as they played standard church songs about being afraid of God and the heavy weight of crosses. She already knew fear and knew the heft of crosses to bear. My mother wanted a celebration at her funeral, smiles. Deborah knew death removes beauty from the vehicle sustaining life; the way our culture gathers to view the bodies of deceased loved ones made her stomach knot.

"That's not my grandmother," I remembered her saying, standing over Mamaw's casket, when I was sixteen. "My grandmother was happier than that. It's morbid to fawn over the dead."

I thought the same things about my mother last night. She had not had a lover in eighteen years but her viewing was on Valentine's Day. Large brown amoeba-shaped spots anointed the backs of her hands from her wrists to her fingers. They were a road map of menopause and twenty years of heavy medication. The coarse wrinkles that surrounded her bad eye have relaxed, no longer straining to keep control. Her skin seemed translucent. Dirty-blond hair, never longer than her shoulders during her life, rested on top of her robust frame. A foreign language of makeup had been applied to her features. Heavier than she would have liked, the blush had slid down the sunken slope of her cheeks and puddled in the folds of her neck.

This is not my mom.

This morning the lid is sealed, as she wanted it. The box is a light pecan color, simple in design. Just like her. The faux natural lighting of the chapel provides an artificial serenity. The wood cross, just as artificial, hovers at the head of the room as the focal point of this House of God. It seems to me presumptuous and out of place. The only holy thing in here is the sunlight; the beams angle down through the stained-glass window above her coffin.

The sliding accordion wall on the right crinkles back. Opened, it reveals rows of folding chairs and benches. The haphazard, mismatched arrangement suggests hurry. They also expected a big crowd. Surrounded by two hundred empty seats, I fear no one else is coming.

"I'm sorry you died alone." Guilt runs over me. "I should have been there." I sit talking as if her spirit lingers around the coffin. "I was not there for you like I should have been."

In truth, our whole relationship was a series of missed connections. I think about the loving way Freeda picked my mom up at work after a seizure and took her home. Freeda made the frequent trips to the emergency room. When my mom moved to Ft. Worth, to be closer to TCU where she finally attended college, I never helped. The resentment of my childhood kept me from the role as a helpful son. Early in my life I needed her, but she was too young, too involved in her twenties to see me through the headaches, her friends, and the depression. Later in her life she needed me, but I was too angry to be concerned. She fell silent. I fell short.

"I wish you would've shown up more." I regret having told her to stop making surprise visits. "You never needed to call, you're my mom." I see my selfishness. I was too busy with my own life to give her respect.

I remember the unhappiness of her life before the surgery. She did not. My resentment didn't permit second chances. Her memory did not hold onto regrets. I was proud of her accomplishments; the only ill words I spoke about her I spoke *to* her. Our whole family knew what a bitch Deb could be, and we teased each other at family gatherings. Betty Bitch was her nickname. She boasted of living up to it. Nine times out of ten, she won her arguments. You could never tell her she was wrong.

"You remember bursting through the bathroom door, the Friday night you had to leave happy hour?" I speak directly to the coffin. A common story for us to share, we traded laughter at our shortcomings, our bonds forged in yelling and pain. Now our bonding is the ghostless air of this sanctuary.

She had called Ann to pick me up and let me spend the night while she went out. She did not tell me. When Ann came by our home to pick me up, I was not there. Debbie's plans interrupted, Ann told her it was not her job to hunt for me. She came home in a fury. I was ten, and it was the last time I cried when my mother hit me.

"I swear you didn't tell me Ann was picking me up. Why else would I have been at Clark's house?" I try to justify my position, twenty-seven years and one dead participant after the fact. "I thought you were going to kill me," I chuckle. "Remember, you told me—you would calm down if I just unlocked the door." I pause for a moment, drifting back to that day. I stood in the bathroom for over twenty minutes; she tried to break through the door. She lost her mind several times in the process. "All I remember are the hands around my neck the moment I unlocked the door." The laughter turns to a stutter. "Wh-why did we always f-fight?"

The echo of my question rings through the beams of the vaulted ceiling. Startled by my own voice, I break my communion with the dead. I hear voices mingling at the entry of the long hallway leading to the chapel. The pallbearers have started to arrive. I hear my uncles shaking hands with them as they receive instructions and red roses for their lapels from the staff. Freeda is asking for me.

"Anyone seen Jason?"

The rest of my immediate family, dressed in bright colors, have gathered in a conference room back in the business offices. Expertly, the staff adorned in top-dollar suits and rehearsed sales-pitch smiles, shuffled us into this cramped space as soon as we arrived, two hours before the ceremony. They make me uncomfortable. Condolence muffins and Sam's Club bottled water in hand, the salespeople told us to just relax.

"It's best if the guests don't see us before we make our entrance into the service," one of the grief-relief team members suggested.

"I'm not staying here. I need air," I said as I left.

We are not the bride and groom at a wedding, nor the graduating class, nor the champion coming out of the dressing room. They want to parade us as people of note, dressed in nice suits and respectful demeanors. I never liked parades. I never liked salespeople. I like being alone.

"Anyone seen Jason?" my grandmother continues.

"He's not in the bathroom," one of my cousins offers.

"He might be outside smoking. He likes to walk around, check his car," Craig interjects. Over the years, Craig and I have remained close. He is a private investigator, a proper citizen, a homeowner in a good community, and a loving family man to his wife and kid. I never would have survived this life without him. "Tell him I'm here when you find him."

I hesitate before joining them. The memories of the four funerals I have already attended in my life come back as I sit in the chapel across from my mother's remains. It seems like death is the only thing that brings our whole family together these days. I run through the series of greetings and hugs I received upon reconnecting with family members, most of who have become strangers over the years. I dread the platitudes.

Don't worry, she is in heaven. She is with Mamaw and Papaw. Deb is not sick anymore. Your mother loved you. She was too young to die. She lived a good life. She is at peace and not struggling.

Everyone whose hands I will shake today will utter at least two of these statements. I prepare myself for this uncomfortable inevitability, less than half an hour away.

Funerals are about lessons. What can you take from the story of the deceased's life? I knew what lessons I had taken from the lives of the dead. I laid to rest my mamaw, her life of hard work and love. Then my mother's sister, Aunt Barbra, died in 1984. Her death taught me the importance of angels. Every time I step onto a stage to perform, I ask the universe to allow her spirit to be present with me. My grandfather went next; he gave me my ability to see into situations, and the goal of never putting off my dreams. All things can vanish in an instant. Papaw's death was about going home. Now my mother, her death is about rest and the victory of surrender. The selfishness of my pain blocks the truth those closest to her want to speak.

"Jason, you okay?" My grandmother Freeda stands at the glass doorway of the chapel. "Honey, you need to come back here now."

"Just checking things out." I shift, uncomfortable, anxious. "You think she would like this?"

"Hon, it is beautiful. It was her time, Jase."

"I have a hard time seeing fifty-four as her time," I say, standing. "That is being robbed of life." I stare at the flower arrangement that covers the top of the coffin.

Freeda buried her youngest daughter twenty-three years ago. This is the second child she has buried. Remarkably, she looks unfazed.

I was fourteen when we buried Aunt Barbra; an aneurysm in her head burst two days after she gave birth to my cousin Robbie. My grandmother awoke to a strange, muffled cry. She went downstairs to discover the horror of Barbra slouched over, one of her large breasts crushing her newborn son, pinned nursing deep within her lap. Freeda struggled to free him from her seized-up unconscious daughter. Barbra held on for two weeks in the ICU.

The night we said goodbye, her whole family gathered around her. Her eyes scoured our faces, unable to speak, her blue eyes desperate and pleading for remembrance beyond what brief moments we shared here. Her half smile connected with mine; as a fourteen-year-old I could only wince and look away. I could not ease her pain, and the limitations of this life were too uncomfortable. I did not want to take it on. An inability to face her gaze haunted me for years. I recognize this same pain in my grandmother when we speak of Barbra. Freeda still cries for her with a guilt-riddled mourning, knowing she too looked away.

"I am sorry Deb's life ended so early." Freeda smiles.

"Mom was blessed," I say, not believing the words.

"Sissy and now Deb. With Sis it was so quick; we had no time to prepare . . . We could feel it hanging around with Deb. Your mom lived longer than she . . . We got lucky to keep her." Tears swell and roll down her face. "She changed after her surgery—more focused and responsible." She pauses. "Didn't remember a damn thing, though." We both laugh just a little as she dries her eyes.

Freeda wears her Sunday suit, a light top trimmed in blue with a dark blue skirt. A large flower that smells of an old woman's perfume is pinned to her chest. Her hair has not changed in thirty-five years. Short and a not-so-natural brown, its color and style elevate her smile. Smiling is one of her strengths. Practiced in the art of dignity, she never shows the scars sewn upon her heart.

"Hey, look there, Jason, what just pulled into the parking lot. Oh my Lord, praise God."

A large yellow school bus unloads its passengers in the parking lot. Teachers and students from West Mesquite High School have come to pay final respects to my mom.

"Look how many kids there are," she says.

One after another they file off the bus in nice dresses and button-down shirts, all of them celebrating the life of Mrs. B.

"She would want you to be honest today, when you speak about her," she tells me, brushing the side of my head with her hand. "She was proud of you."

I grasp her hand, the skin spotted and clammy. Her arms are heavy and fragile. She is shrinking. For the first time, I see her as an old woman. I start to cry.

The totality of my mother's life comes over me. She conquered adversity—depression, domestic violence, epilepsy, migraines, asthma, and surgery for an aneurysm—more than most people could face. She went to college, fulfilled her dreams. A high school teacher in the district that made her drop out when she got pregnant. My mother not only taught political science, she also educated people to live to their fullest potential.

Pride overcame me in joyful tears. What she was unable to give me early in life she made amends for in the lives of other children. This was my mother, a great and awkward woman. She never asked for mercy.

* * *

The sky is the brightest blue. The day looks like eighty-five degrees, but the temperature is twenty-seven. Everyone waits in the vehicles for the pallbearers to take their places. Spring a few weeks away, the fierce bite of the wind shakes the leafless branches.

This act is one of the greatest things you can do for a person, I think, watching the six men I chose to carry my mother's coffin. A stoic purpose upon their faces, they bring it to the awaiting grave. Everyone steps out into the freezing February blue-sky sun.

All of the flowers situated around the coffin, under a tent with folding chairs but no walls, fight with the elements. A few potted plants blow over. The large flower wreaths that stand on tripods launch their blooms like colorful rockets into the jet stream of wind, across the tent with its temporary Astroturf carpet. A large branch falls from a fir tree to the right, landing on the car parked beneath it. We all huddle close together, creating a shield, deflecting the wind as we say our goodbyes.

"Consecrate this body . . ." the pastor speaks. He has never met my mother.

The simple prayer lasts three minutes and the graveside service ends. The crowd leaves quickly; only the closest of family and friends remain. The conversations turn to catching up on each other's lives and less about remembrances of Deb. We discuss the proper way to mourn after a funeral— margaritas and Mexican food. My mouth grows dry with the everyday-life feeling that takes over the family members left at the tent; uncomfortable in my suit, I remember the change of clothes I brought for after the service. I fear this uncomfortable-suit sensation will hang on me the rest of my life. I watch as cars filled with students file out of the cemetery, their faces smiling, their heads swaying with the song on the radio.

She will stay here, I think. I catch myself in the tragic false hope of flesh. She is gone, not here.

One of the large yellow school buses backfires as it rounds the curve toward the front gate; it startles the birds that scatter off in a frenzy. I think about the ride over from the funeral home. Each automobile had its headlights turned on, and drove slowly, in an unbroken chain, the procession escorted by rent-a-cops on Harley-Davidson motorcycles stretched back as far as I could see. We rolled through all the intersections, headed toward the highway. Total strangers, who normally flip you off for going too slowly or cutting them off, pulled over and patiently waited for the friends and family of the deceased to pass. I found it funny that one of the few times in a person's life where your race, religion, gender, sexual orientation, or class means nothing is at funerals. We lay each other to rest with the respect deserved by all humans.

The day unfolded beyond my wildest expectations. We celebrated Deborah.

Now I look at the ground around her grave; the markers for family members whom I knew from my youth surround us.

Grandma and Grandpa Arnold over there, my grandfather's parents. They died when I was young. He used to do a magic trick where he pulled quarters from my ears.

Aunt Millie and Uncle Clyde. She was a mean drunk who used to call from Arkansas late at night to cuss out whomever picked up the phone. "Goddamn son-of-a-bitch asshole, put J.W. on the fucking phone, smart-ass kid," she'd told me one night when I was eight, upon saying hello.

I thought about Millie's old age, after J.W. and Clyde had died. All alone and sick, my grandmother helped her move down to Mesquite and took care of this vile woman. The years of drinking and anger withered Millie into a feeble and sickly ghost of a person. She proved what you reap is what you sow. She rented an apartment down the street from Freeda and sat at Freeda's dining table more than her own. I found her one night in the upstairs hall bathroom. She'd defecated all over herself and the floor, sobbing, in another world. *"Where is my mommy? I need my mommy,"* her voice echoed through my head.

She thought I was her father. Her whole body caved and flinched away from my arms as I went to help. It took Freeda to convince her I was not going to hit her. I saw the damage that caused her sickness: the birthplace within her mind where hostility formed, her burden expelled all over the white tile and cream grout. My grandmother and I washed that woman. We both found her hard to stomach.

My mom will rest between Barbra and J.W. Both graves are now covered by dug-up dirt and Astroturf, under where we stand. My mom will not burden anyone, she will not grow old and sick like Millie. For the first time in her life, she is safe.

Tears driven by the wind are forced across the surface of my eyes. My vision blurs, colder than regret. I take in as much as I can. I resolve not to return here. Some people believe in flowers at gravesides, conversations held with tombstones, thinking that if you cling to flesh it resurrects loved ones. I do not. As my family gathers up the arrangements and plants to take with us, I know I do not need a graveside to speak with my mother.

She is finally at peace, resting far away in what I choose to call heaven. Far away from this box on the stand, far from the seizures and migraines that drove her flesh into this earth, and far from this feeling of remorse and regret that has brought me to this grim cemetery for a cold, last goodbye with her empty vessel. I grab a handful of roses off the casket and awkwardly walk away.

SIMPLE MOMENTS
1981

"MERRY CHRISTMAS! SANTA HAS COME," my mom says.

She wakes me with a smile. The edges of the pillow are cold. I turn my head and look up at the ceiling. A faint chill seeps from the window above my bed. The cold room is full of light—the white walls have an extra-clean sheen this morning. The heated air from the vent ripples as it touches the frost of the room. I am wide awake two seconds after I hear her voice.

I am eleven years old and I no longer believe in Santa. She knows this. We both pretend to recapture some lost moment when I was a small boy and still believed.

"Santa's here!" I shout.

Before she can say another word, I am out of the bed, hurling myself down the stairs, two at a time.

I smell her coffee brewing in the Mr. Coffee as I reach the bottom step. She loves coffee. I love the aroma and my mom's elegant appearance when she drinks a cup.

I get most of my ideas from television. The people in the commercials are all successful sophisticates who embrace the challenges of the day, while they stare out at the snow-covered ski slopes, happy with their white-teeth smiles. I crave my mom's happiness. I smile knowing she will enjoy my gifts—a five-dollar bottle of grocery-store perfume and a coffee mug. The sound of the coffee trickling, one droplet at a time into the pool of the carafe, gives me comfort. The room feels fresh and alive.

The miniblinds on the living room window are open. The world outside resembles an ice cube. An ice storm is as close to a white Christmas as Big D gets and stillness looms over the day. The car windshield looks like shattered glass, as a sheet of ice radiates fractures across its surface. The large green electrical box in the front yard has clumps of ice draping over its constant hum. The way the ice freezes, trapped in a slow trickle down the smooth surface, I imagine the box to be a huge holiday cake. The sensations of winter stir over me. I am in no hurry today.

"Where do you want to start?" she asks.

"I'll pass them out, Deb," I say.

The fact that I call her by her name does not always bother her. My mother enjoys the thought of us being confidantes. She loves when salespeople mistake her for my older sister. She relishes the attention that comes from having your brother and not your son on your arm in public. Men often hit on her with this error in thinking; she is never quick to correct them. The way she readily accepts their flirtations with an innocent smile intrigues me to no end. I often play along. For those brief moments, she can be a twenty-something young woman not saddled with a half-grown child. She thinks the reason she cannot find a decent man is that guys do not want to date women with baggage. I think good men are hard to find drunk in a bar or naked in a strange bed. I am not as naïve as she thinks.

My mom sits on the couch. Her green velour robe with a zipper running down the front droops under the mess of loose blond curls that cascade lopsided from her head. She wears this robe more than anything else she owns. She has headaches about four days a week. Home by six in the evening, she is in the robe five minutes later. Then she stretches out on the couch until her medication kicks in around eight thirty or nine. The bright peach and pink flowers of the couch clash with the green robe as she sleeps. On those days when she does not feel bad, she hits happy hour after work; some nights until nine or ten, other nights she does not come home at all. Her schedule, like most things in her life, is very erratic.

The tension in her face is not recognizable. This morning, her eyes appear to be the same size. When she has headaches, her right eye swells, closes tight, and waters as if something behind it has squeezed all the liquid out. If she has a hangover, her makeup cascades down her cheeks, reminders of late-night prayers into the toilet. I have heard her begging Jesus to give her back her legs. She thought herself paralyzed one night last month from the waist down and lay in her own vomit. I feel bad that I laughed. My loyalty to her rarely waivers; I have become a good reader of her signs. Today, I know she feels sane. This morning she belongs to me.

She lights up a cigarette. The gray sunlight illuminates her exhales. The air inside our home is grimy with a layer of smoke. The dust of its residue covers most of our furniture, saturates our clothes. I dislike that she smokes, urge her to quit; she never gives me that gift. I pass out the six presents. Two for her and four for me; I feel guilty that I did not give her more.

"Shit, the cinnamon rolls," she says as she darts into the kitchen. "Wait just a second."

I study the Christmas packages. Each wrapped tightly— my mother has a knack for ribbons, bows, and tape. She damn near makes them impenetrable. Yet she cannot disguise the sound of the contents as I shake them. Two are definitely clothes, each bulky enough to contain a pair of pants or a sweater.

Typical.

My mother uses my birthday in June as an excuse to give

me a couple of summer outfits every year. Christmas is when I get the other two outfits of new school clothes. She has a talent for combining my presents with things that I need anyway.

I bet one of these is some dress clothes for today.

One of the other two sounds like a board game.

Great, I think, *some little-kid game.*

The contents rattle like a thousand-piece puzzle; the package is the appropriate weight.

I hate jigsaw puzzles.

The last is unknown, which I like best. A medium-sized square, ten inches long, ten inches deep, ten inches wide. When I shake the box, it makes no sound, a good, balanced weight, not too heavy but definitely not clothes. I am excited that I have no idea what is inside. On each package is a holiday sticker that tells who the gift is for and who gave the present. All of my packages say, *From Santa,* in my mom's handwriting.

She is so retarded.

She sings "Silent Night" in the kitchen while she frosts the rolls. Pillsbury cinnamon rolls are her idea of a weekend breakfast. She knows how to make eggs and bacon, hash browns. We eat breakfast for dinner two nights a week. She never cooks breakfast for breakfast. I do not understand this.

I look through the branches of the tree. Stare off into the light of the patio. The needles muddle together in the foreground as I focus on the pavement. The ice sheet reminds me of the rough bumpy grain of ostrich-skin boots. I can practically feel the frozen wet chill of the surface with my eyes. My body shivers warm, I retreat to the lights of the tree. We always get a real tree; always decorate the pine needles the same way—red and silver glass balls hang over strings of white blinking lights covered in fuzzy aluminum garlands and silver icicles. By the time we finish, the whole thing looks fake.

My grandparents' tree is artificial. A revolving color wheel sits on the plush red tree skirt with an embroidered Santa Claus face. The wheel underneath the tree at the back points up. As it spins, silver icicles hanging from the plastic needles shimmer blue and green, red and orange, the living room of their house becoming a plastic-covered-couch discotheque. My mom learned early that white-trash people, trying to look expensive, do gaudy best.

"Hurry!" I shout into the kitchen. After all, it is Christmas morning.

"They're ready. Come and get some! Milk or orange juice?"

"Dr. Pepper," I say, heading down the hall. I drink more soda than anything else.

I always get the middle cinnamon roll. That specific roll is the prime one—all the edges soft and moist, the icing runs into the middle of the cluster, coats the top like a glacier. A paper plate with three rolls and a DP in hand, I head back to the tree.

I sit cross-legged in front of my presents, my breakfast on the coffee table to my left. My mom sits on the couch: smokes, drinks coffee, and nibbles on a roll.

"I want to open this one," I say, mouth full of food, pointing to one of the boxes of clothes.

"Sure," she smiles. She has always liked to dress me up as if I was some kind of Ken doll. I hate her taste in clothes.

I shovel the second half of the roll into my still-full mouth. I chew vigorously to make room for air. I lick my fingers clean. Take a gulp of soda. Pick up the package and struggle with the ribbon. I tear Frosty the Snowman and elves with candy canes, discard the paper to the floor. The white box is taped on all sides.

I hand her the box without even trying to open the flimsy film adhesive. My mother offers a fingernail and promptly gets a paper cut.

"Shit," she says. "Fuck me. Debbie, you should know better. Let me get a knife."

I can't wait that long. I grab the box and rip a spot along the edge of the top between the tape and the corner. The top peels back, I can see the white tissue paper.

"I got it!" I yell.

She comes back out of the kitchen, butter knife in hand, laughing at my impatience. I remove the tissue.

"A sweater and some jeans," I say with a surprised look on my face.

"That isn't all," she says, as she stands behind me.

I reach into the box. There is nothing else in there.

"Look on the pants."

"Oh, a belt," I say in a less-than-surprised way.

"What do you think? It's your Christmas Day outfit." She smiles with triumph and hands me the butter knife for the rest of the presents, then returns to the couch.

A gray sweater with big aqua diamonds on the front, a pair of black pants with matching black belt: an excellent outfit for going to church on Sundays or to an important family gathering.

Gross.

She smiles endlessly as I hold up the clothes to my body to check the size.

I am a dress-up doll in an ugly sweater.

I know I have to wear it later today. We are going to Mamaw and Papaw's house for lunch. I have to look my best for the gala of paper plates and casseroles.

"I like it a lot. Thanks, Mom. Your turn."

She opens her present. This is not as much fun for her; she prefers watching me open mine. I love the moments when

I can do something nice for her. The package not bound so neatly, she opens hers without pause.

"Oh, perfume, my favorite." The look on her face tells me that the gift does not matter, whatever brand it happens to be; the important thing is that the gift was from me. "Thank you, Jason." By the time she gets that out of her mouth, I am opening the second boxes of clothes. The butter knife makes my job easy.

"All right! A Michigan sweatshirt and a pair of jeans," I say, honestly excited, they are my favorite college team. Strange for a kid from Texas, I watch Michigan football every Saturday afternoon in the fall. Sure, I like UT, the Longhorns are my family's favorite. Earl Campbell achieves Muhammad Ali or Hank Aaron status around our Sunday supper conversations. They call him by name. The truth is my grandmother and I watch University of Michigan football together on Saturdays when I spend the night; I like the team mainly for the time I get with my grandma and for the helmets. Every Christmas I receive a new University of Michigan sweatshirt. My mom thinks I will go to law school there; I think I'll be playing football there until the Dallas Cowboys draft me. Neither one of us knows yet how much of a pipe dream this is.

"You open another one," she says.

I make a move for the square box. Her eyes brighten and I can tell this is the big present. Solid two or three minutes to undo the bow, ribbons, and wrapping paper. Tape is four layers deep along the edges of the box.

She must go through four or five rolls per gift.

I struggle to pull the plain brown box apart. I can now hear the rattle of the contents. What sounds like one solid object moves from side to side, as I fight with the adhesive. I can tell it takes up most of the box. I reach inside and pullout a telephone. My eyes light up.

"A telephone!" I cry out, excitement overcoming me. I begin to rip through the packaging, removing the plastic and twist ties that hold it all together.

When my mom's eyes fall on me in pleased ways, a feeling of contentment comes over me that I cannot describe. So much of her life has been turmoil and pain. I just want her to be happy.

"There are a couple of different stickers inside the box," she explains. "You can change them as often as you want. They have all kinds of sports team and television show decals you can get for it." She laughs. "You can even get one with Fonzie. Answer the phone *HEEEYYY!*" Her imitation leaves a lot to be desired.

I ignore her. My focus is on the telephone, a large white square, with the receiver on the left and the number pad to the right. The flat surface of the top is blue with a big gray star. A Dallas Cowboys decal already covers the entire top of the phone, which looks very modern and cool. I search through the box and pull out two more sports decals. The whole idea of having a phone in my room is very exciting to me.

This is a big-kid present for sure.

I take a few minutes to study my new phone. Pick up the receiver, act as if I am talking with someone. The phone is lightweight. The number pad is push-button, not rotary like most of our other phones have been. I feel like a teenager with it in my hand. I forget about the other present still in its wrapping. I plug the phone into the wall and listen to the dial tone.

"This is so great," I say. "Thanks, Mom, a lot."

"You have one more to open."

"You first," I say, still playing with the phone.

She grabs the second of her gifts. The obvious shape clings to the comic section of newspaper that I used for wrapping paper. She fakes excitement well as she opens it.

"Oh good, a new coffee mug," she smiles, "I need one of these."

The mug is black and has quotes from Shakespeare on the front. *To be or not to be* is the first one. I thought the mug appropriate, considering my mom's trouble with that question. It has been two years since she last tried to swallow pills and ended up in the mental ward of the hospital. Our life has not changed much. I have moved four times since that night, I have changed schools three times, but we have been together. We spent last year living in this same complex with her friend Pam. Then they got into a fight over money and we moved in here. This rented town house is only the second home we have had that was all ours; I like it even though most nights are lonely.

"All right, last present," she says, looking at her watch.

I grab the box and shake it to draw out the suspense. "I wonder what this could be. A jigsaw puzzle?"

"You hate those," she says.

I tear the paper. When the main fold comes undone, I can see the back of a board game. I remove the rest of the paper, flip the box over.

"Scrabble?" I say.

"It's an adult game. You love words and language so much, poetry and your big vocabulary, I thought you would enjoy this."

An adult game sounds boring. *What a waste.* She did remember I like words, but I like Dungeons & Dragons and the handheld Electronic Quarterback video game more.

"Thanks, Mom," I say, feeling a bit unsatisfied. I conceal my feelings with a large kiss and a hug.

"Are you sure you like them, Jason?"

"Yes, Mom. I'm going to call Craig right now," I say.

Craig and I have a tradition. Every Christmas morning I call him after I open my presents and we discuss what Santa had delivered. I live vicariously through Craig. He always gets cool stuff; Aunt Annie gives the best gifts. Our moms are both single. Yet there is something different about him. Not the fact that he is a year and nine months older, not the fact that he is the youngest grandchild while I am the oldest great-grandchild. He is comfortable being himself. I recognize in him what I lack. He is everything I want to be; I imitate his actions, his sayings, and the things he is into. His favorites become mine. He is meticulous and clean, his room is always spotless.

In my room, there are no posters on the white walls. A dark walnut desk my mother bought for me when we rented this place is the focal point. The dark stain and brass knobs seem more suited to an office or study than a ten-year-old's bedroom. The window above my bed has Budweiser Beer Budman curtains, which belonged to whoever lived here last. My bed belongs to my dead great-great-grandmother. The bed smells like Grandma Spades—dusty body powder and grit. The blanket on top has white pearls of fabric intertwined with the fancy woven cotton top. She made this blanket with her buckled hands. In her bitter old age, her arthritic knuckles were the only frail part of her. At least that is what my family says.

She is in my dreams. We talk feverishly about things I do not understand. I get the sense that she loves me dearly; the fact that I dream of this old dead woman bothers me. I never say anything about my dreams or feelings, scared they will put me into the crazy bin like my mom. I live in silence, uncomfortable about the bed I sleep heavy in and the old woman who does not bother me but will not leave me alone. My only memory of her is not really a memory at all. A framed black-and-white photograph sits on Papaw's end table. A five-generation image holds the lineage that shapes me. I do not understand the emotion that the grains of the image stir inside my heart. I sit in that old woman's lap barely nine months old. When I am at my great-grandparents' house, I stare lost at the photograph for hours. The love trapped under the glass is magical.

My mom crouches behind me on the floor as I start to dial Craig's number. She squeezes me tightly, an exhale of happiness slow out of her lungs. I hang up the phone and she hugs me as if she is never letting go.

"Why don't you try on your clothes?" she asks.

"Let's play a game before we get ready to go," I say.

"You go try on the pants and I'll set up the game." She lets go and moves back to her coffee cup.

I stand up, fetch the pants out of the box, head upstairs. I have a good feeling about today.

The smell of the ice on the roof invades the bright shadow of the gray morning that hangs over my room. The room is crisp; Grandma Spades's blanket glistens.

The phone should go there on the desk.

I struggle with the black cotton pants. "They're too tight!" I yell down from my bed.

"Shit, I knew they would be," she calls back. "Take them off. We'll bring them back."

Downstairs, I study the top of the board game. The pink and blue squares are intriguing and there's a large star in the center. There are no rooms to move pieces into, no elaborate maze of contraptions to construct before trying to snare a plastic mouse. There are no pictures of children falling down ladders into large bins of apples, no dome-covered dice tray that makes annoying sounds every time it is pressed.

This looks really cool.

The board is elegant, a large grid resembling a giant SOS board that we draw on paper in school. Along one edge are the letters of the alphabet with a numerical value out to the right of each.

"What does that mean?" I ask.

"It tells you how many of each letter there are in the game," she explains. "More common letters have more tiles, less common letters like Q and J have only one tile."

"That makes sense," I say.

"You draw seven letters. The object is to create words that build off your opponent's words using your seven letters. Each letter has a value that you total at the end of each turn."

"Okay."

She hands me a piece of wood from the box. "Use this to hold your tiles." She smiles.

Over the next three minutes, she explains the rest of the rules. They seem straightforward enough; nothing about this game says *little kid*. I am still unsure of whether I like it or not. My mother seems very happy to be playing this with me; I am happy to have her attention.

"Draw seven tiles," she says. "Don't let me see them."

Pine-colored chips; I can't tell if the small squares are wood or imitation. Each has a black letter etched into the grain. I stack my letters in alphabetical order, separating the consonants from the vowels. I study the tiles, come up with three different three-letter words.

This does seem difficult.

The main challenge is that while my vocabulary is quite large, I do not know how to spell most of the words I know.

"You go first," she offers. "One of your letters has to be on the black star."

H-O-M-E. I place my tiles on the board. Her eyes light up, we smile at one another.

"Double word score," she says. "Draw four new tiles out of the box top. Let's take our time, enjoy our morning."

Even at this young age, I know these moments are timeless.

THIS IS THE LONGEST RED LIGHT IN HISTORY.

Tonight, C asked me to do him a favor. I will receive a free forty bag of dope to go with the two hundred I bought. All I have to do is take this long-nailed whore to the complex half a mile away. The early morning is dark and hollow. This is a place I avoid even in the sunlight. She carries her purse tightly to her chest, as if her life depends on her arrival.

Our destination is the shadiest of habitats on this side of Dallas. The BV apartment complex, open for business for forty years, is fifty feet off the corner of Buckner and John West, two hundred feet from where we idle, trapped at the light at Peavey.

"I don't like having that shit in my car," I mutter as we wait.

"You got paid, quit bugging."

Something is not right, the street hovers at a hush. I sift over my reflection in the rearview mirror. A strain of insomnia shows in my death-mask grin. My slow demise is cruel and bitter to those who love me. I chase myself, endlessly. I trade everything I love for the greed, the gnawing compulsions of what I have grown to hate. The smudged yellow lamps silhouetting Buckner Boulevard hang over the asphalt like the bones of a half-eaten carcass. The entrance to the crack houses behind the strip mall and Burger King is a ghastly image of carnivorous and unyielding sickness.

Entering these complexes is treacherous, especially if you

can't sort which gangster to deal with among the hordes of zombies. Ignorant victims buy fake dope, slivers of almonds or soap, in tightly sealed plastic. Sometimes exiting, undercover cops pull them over. It's easy to be stupid here, robbed of life or money before getting out. Young black males strap up with a powerless, genocidal ignorance holstering their dreams. In every direction of this stretch of Dallas, gangsters strangle false-idol affections of love through dope, guns, and money. Not even their family members escape the addictive pursuit of pay. The venerable tradition of overconsumption covers every inch of concrete, every minute of every hour. Crackheads, streetwalkers, drug dealers, and hustlers all serve different purposes in a slavish and doomed cycle of life.

This neighborhood was left for dead years ago.

The street is a silent corpse tonight, unusual.

I am a wreck more than two decades in the making.

The only thing I recognize in my reflection is the blue of my eyes, diluted to a small halo around the flowered deadness of the dark center.

What the hell am I doing?

"What you staring at? Quit bugging out!" the woman in the passenger seat says. "Muthafucka gonna get me popped!"

"This light takes so fucking long," I say. "C'mon. C'mon, I have shit to do."

"Hmmm," she mutters. "Busy night smoking crack."

"Guess that beats sucking dick for crack. Although there isn't much difference."

Her nails roll over the vinyl middle console in unison with her breath. A twisted hard-shell cackle punctuates the tension. A haggard scar of a person, her peroxide wig sits lopsided on her head. Her fingernails curve so steeply they look like purple claws adorned with red rhinestones and roses made of gold glitter. They are the most expensive thing about her.

"You need to take your ass back to wherever, you smell

like shit." She half laughs looking out her window as it rolls down. "Take a shower. Have some respect, sad-ass white boy."

"You look nice too, just like the first time I saw you."

"You don't know me!" Old Fingernails snaps.

"It's right there, c'mon, change, damnit," I huff.

"*Clockwork*, why he calls you that?" she questions, already knowing the answer. The ill truth of the nickname means I score so frequently and with such a consistent hunger that he can pinpoint within five or ten minutes when I will call or show up. He sets his watch by me, times his middle-of-the-night deliveries accordingly. I constantly do him favors.

"Ha. White boy, you keep time around that muthafucka."

"I used to live there as a kid," I say, pointing to the BV. "Back when the Buckner Boulevard Drive-in Theater was still open."

"You ain't ever stay there," she says. "This is the hood."

"It hasn't always been the hood. But it has always been violent . . . Where the fuck is everybody? The silence is eerie," I change the course of conversation.

"It must be hot out," she says, correlating the lack of activity with a strong police presence.

"I hope not. Why is this light not changing?" I glance around for any sign of squad cars. "This light needs to change, get you out of my car."

There are no illusions here. For a quarter-mile in either direction, the night is quiet and thick. No hustles going down. The remnants of a light rain earlier glaze the roadway. The shine of the silence is almost magical. At night, fast-food outlets bustle selling two-for-a-dollar tacos to drunken carloads of bar refugees. Homeless crackheads work as lookouts for low-level dealers at the gas station parking lot where they also panhandle for change. Streetwalkers cling to their purses for balance, jockeying for position around an invisible track. The haze of oblivion paints their thoroughbred faces, searching for rich johns through rolled-down windows. Everyone who travels this three-mile stretch of road becomes infested with the gravity of the situation, even when all the characters are absent. America pours out of this neighborhood with reckless abandon and need.

"Ignore this light, man, let's go!" she demands.

"Patience, I ain't running shit with that in the car."

"See there, the other side is green."

My knuckles tighten around the steering wheel. I adjust my ass in the seat, anticipating the arrow. The opposite light pole turns yellow, then red.

"What the fuck?" I scream. "Fucking light skipped us! How the hell can it skip us? Hello? Dumb fucking light, there are no other cars on the road!"

Three minutes become five. The stiffness in my expanding jaw urges me to smoke.

"In and out in three minutes," I whisper into the rearview. "I roll in quick, drop her off without parking, make the U-shaped path to the exit. Takes ten minutes to get—"

"What the fuck you mumbling?"

"Planning," I say. "Back to the hotel down Peavey to Garland Road, then left at Jupiter to the interstate. I can be smoking in seventeen minutes."

"Tweaking-ass fiend," she says.

"I need a hit. This fucking light needs to come on—change, you cocksucker, change! This is bullshit," I snap, slamming my hand on the steering wheel.

She jumps. "What the fuck is wrong with you? Get me out of this car. Boy, you need to run this light. Crazy-ass fool."

"Chill," I say. "We're cool."

"We're anything but cool, you're fucked up. You smell like shit. Going to get us busted with your bullshit craziness."

A flash of headlight darts across the cab of the car. Something in our lane is coming up behind us quicker than my thoughts can process.

A car rushes by the open window within a few inches, a black blur. The vehicle launches off the rounded median. By the time I blink and turn to look, a cloud of dust and a jumble of debris have formed in the intersection. The vehicle flings itself end over end, bashes a light pole. A body ejects through the dust storm, slaps the asphalt. Rims with rubber shred off, fly twenty feet into the air. A bumper careens off the concrete, splits into pieces. Shards of fiberglass, glass from windows, windshields, headlights, and bits of metal shoot off in all directions. The body does not bounce. It's a swirling violent explosion as if this is the excitement of a stock car race, where spectators pay to see the collisions more than the victories. The automobile comes to rest upside down on the median.

"Did you just see that? Jesus fucking Christ, it almost hit us!"

"Let's go, let's go!" she screams. "White boy, let's go!"

Def and Confused
2002

Don't play to the cameras, play to the crowd.

The back hallway is silent. The high ceilings hold the hot air down. This space feels like a box overstuffed with Styrofoam peanuts. I find it hard to breathe. I'm nervous as hell.

Make connections with people.

The walls vibrate from the laughter of the audience, somewhere on the other side, as the comedian warming up the crowd rolls through his set. I've never been on television. This whole weekend is way over my head. Russell Simmons's *Def Poetry* attracts some big-name celebrities: Kanye West, Mos Def, Dave Chappelle, Amiri Baraka . . . What am I doing here?

Shit. I cannot remember my poem. What is my poem?

"*My Southern heritage . . .*" I mumble, trying to recall the words.

The poets in the small greenroom speak in loud whispers. I hear their echoes through a cracked metal door. They seem so relaxed. Their calm conversations make me more nervous. In fifteen minutes, I will be on stage. Right now, I can only remember the first three words to this damn poem.

This taping is one of the most crammed in the shooting schedule, loaded with veteran talent. Beau Sia, one of my favorites, wears a hot-pink cashmere sweater. His performance style is in-your-face, political, and very funny. He is a Broadway cast member of *Def Poetry*. I figure that if I rock the crowd as hard as he will, then I should be all right. Easier said than done. We don't have the same flare. I wear a black T-shirt with a logo from Blaze 1, a bong-making glassblower in Chico, California.

"*My Southern heritage . . .*" I repeat, staring at the ground. My mind constructs patterns in the porous, chipped concrete. Lynyrd Skynyrd lyrics keep popping in my head: *Big wheels keep on turning . . . Carry me home to see my kin . . . Singing songs about the Southland . . .*

"I'm not from Alabama," I tell myself. I light a smoke. Nerves have never been this much of a problem for me.

I try to believe the anxious stirring my stomach is telling me that I am ready, the nervous energy storing itself up for the imminent release. Once I hit the stage, the energy will take over and carry the breath of the poem out of my body. When I'm really connected, I can't remember what I did on stage. The tingling sensation is the same as writing. I see the act of creation as the universe giving me medicine to heal myself, while the act of performing is the universe using me to take that medicine and heal someone else. I learned a long time ago that you only get to keep what you're willing to give away, but you can't give away what you don't have.

I feel like I am going to explode. I walk in small circles, going nowhere, retracing my steps; every time I pass the large green trash can, I take a drag. I try to run the lines of my poem. Again, I can't get past the first three words. And Lynyrd Skynyrd lyrics fill my head. My body aches, clenched up with energy. My mind, cluttered with nonsense, is empty to the task at hand. Everything seems surreal and out of place. I turn away from the door.

"*Sweet home Alabama, Lord I'm coming home to you . . .*" I mumble through the filter of smoke in my mouth.

I follow the hallway fifty feet to a small three-step concrete staircase. It's not until I reach the stairwell that I realize I'm singing the chorus to that damn song again. My Aunt Barbra turned me on to Lynyrd Skynyrd. She loved rock music and rock stars. She died at thirty, never got to live her dreams.

I remember the last time I saw her alive, the way her eyes trapped me. In a bed, unable to move her limbs, her eyes made the only physical connection she could. When I was six, some kids chased me home, trying to beat me up. She stomped out the backdoor as they caught up with me in the unfenced yard. All four foot eleven of her barked like a rabid beast. She loved me. She was the first person to ever sit and listen to one of my poems; encouraged me to enter a silly thing in the cultural art contest at school. She would be proud of me.

Tonight, I read for her. I want to sing the song of my family.

The memories of Aunt Barbra calm me; the clutter in my head dissipates. I want to be here for the right reasons. I know I can't fail. This is who I am. Who I was always meant to be.

BLOOD RUNS DOWN HIS FOREARM, pooling in his palm. The skin is peeled back, exposing what appear to be the bones of his hand. I crouch at the driver's-side window, reaching out to touch the young man on the forearm. Shirtless and tattooed, his body type is identical to the driver lying on the concrete. I cannot tell if his short hair is naturally black, or if the darkness is blood. I smell gasoline as it trickles from the tank. The possibility of a spinal injury worries me more than the car bursting into flames. His head tilts to the side, pressed against the roof, his seat belt suspending him upside down in the middle of the crumpled cab. The wheeze of his breath releases a gurgle of liquid. I do not dare release him.

"I'm right here," I utter. "You're not alone. You're going to be fine."

He does not seem to be conscious, but his labored breathing reveals his struggle. I do not know what to do. I stand up look over the wreckage. At the far sidewalk, the crowd stands watching. No one does anything. The driver of the car is still in the street, my T-shirt under his head.

"Where are the fire trucks?" I yell.

No one responds.

I squat back down to the young man. His palm is missing most of its skin. Ridges of bones track through the blood. Neither of his upper limbs appears to be broken. I am not so sure about his neck and back. The roof of the car bends inward in rounded arcs. The cabin is half of its original size.

He struggles to breathe. I keep noticing the same things, one to the next, none of them change. Each second grows more desperate. I am in over my head.

"I'm right here. Ambulance is on its way," I say.

I feel helpless. I have nothing to offer in this situation. I look at my car. I can just drive away, leave others to their own problems. Fingernails is gone.

My dope is probably gone as well.

I do not really care at this point, any minute this street will be full of firefighters and cops. They probably won't be able to save him.

"Your family loves you," I say. "They love you more than anything."

I do not know if this is true. Those are the words I wish my mother had heard as she fell from life. My being carries a sense of calamity, which has been following me since her death. But right now, for the first time in weeks, I don't feel paranoid. I don't care about the dope. Pursuing a mission of overdose and death since the funeral gives in to more of the loneliness I have embraced my whole life. I only care about going home, leaving this neighborhood where my family once lived. Here I learned faith and how to fight for what I believed, even if sometimes those things were the wrong things. This is the neighborhood where my mother died.

"Your life is a great gift to them," I continue. "They love you very much. You are a great gift to them."

Each of his exhales bubbles. His breath is faint and shallow. I stroke his arm as if he were my child. I feel helpless, selfish for not knowing what to do.

Do not die on me.

"Your family is proud of you, they love you very much."

I expect him to expire, to go that place on the other side of the thin veil we cannot see. I wonder what thoughts are in his head.

Can he hear me?

My hand reaches out and holds his arm, squeezes. He doesn't move.

Where are the fire trucks?

The station is less than a quarter-mile away at S.S. Conner Elementary School. I feel like I have been sitting next to him for hours.

"Your life is a great gift to them, they are so thankful for you and your love. Don't give up. Fight, brother." I am crying and praying. I can feel Ernest and his lessons stirring in my guts. "Heavenly Father, help this man. Reach out to his heart. "

I am asking for myself as much as for this stranger.

The End

Acknowledgments

I encourage everyone to BUNNY UP!

I would like to express a special gratitude to Karen G. and Kate Shuster for their wonderful insights and complete honesty.

Craig, Daylon, Chris, Sean, and Eddy, I ain't got the words for what I feel for y'all.

I would like to thank the following groups, organizations, and persons: Clebo, Gno, Jason Edwards, Bob "Whoopee Cat" Stephens, Rockbaby, Dallas Poetry Slam, Fort Worth Poetry Slam, Seattle Poetry Slam, Tara Hardy, Mike Henry and Phil West, Austin Poetry Slam, Danny Solis, ABQ Poetry Slam, Matthew John Connelly, Laura E.J. Moran, Henry Sampson, Scott Woods, Poetry Slam Inc., Lynne Procope, louderARTS Project NYC, Naz and Dahled, Ekabumi, Oakland and Berkeley Poetry Slams, Taylor Mali, Urbana Poetry Slam NYC, Mo Browne and the Nuyorican Poets Café, Jeanann Verlee, *Union Station* magazine, OKC Slam, Daniel Roop, Amye Archer, Mr. Jim Warner, *Pank*, Marc Smith, Patricia Smith, Roger Bonair-Agard, Ann Morrison, Arley and Judy, Jay and Eddy and their families, Dennis Arnold, Wallace Dunbar, Mr. and Mrs. George Bourgeios, Port Veritas, Will Gibson, Geoff Trenchard, Marty McConnell, Kevin Coval, Bryonn Bain, Greg Polvere, Michael Pavlov, the College Agency, Inkera, Bluz, Carlos Robson, the Asia Project, Katie Wirsing, Bertrand Boyd III, Al Letson, Jeff Kass, Regie Gibson, Gerry Quigley, Jack McCarthy, Ray McNiece, Buddy Wakefield, Beau Sia, Bill MacMillan, Gabrielle Bouliane, Thomas H. and

Allison D., Taz, Mack Dennis, Abdul-Kenyatta, Amy Weaver, Vic, Zach, Stefan, Wilkes University, Dr. Bonnie Culver, Dr. J. Michael Lennon, Susan Cartsonis, Kaylie Jones, Akashic Books, Nancy McKinley, Jaclyn Fowler, Amber Diamonds, Literary Lions, Tracy Tine, Opalina and Carlos, Uncle Brooks and Aunt Joy, Mrs. Collins, Scotty, and the rest of the Collins brothers, Danny H., anyone who has ever given me a place to crash and a spot to perform, and all "slam" poets everywhere.